ALL-AMERICA

ALL AMERICA

THE CATALOGUE OF EVERYTHING AMERICAN

QUILL
WILLIAM MORROW
NEW YORK

A QUARTO BOOK

Copyright © 1987 by Quarto Marketing Ltd.

Library of Congress Catalog Card Number: 86-63662

ISBN: 0-688-07198-8 (trd.)
ISBN: 0-688-07199-6 (pbk.)

ALL-AMERICA: The Catalogue of Everything American
was prepared and produced by
Quarto Marketing Ltd.
15 West 26th Street
New York, N.Y. 10010

Editors: Karla Olson/Louise Quayle
Editorial Assistant: Sharon L. Squibb
Designer: Rod Gonzalez
Photo Editor: Susan M. Duane
Production Manager: Karen L. Greenberg

Typeset by BPE Graphics, Inc.
Color separations by Hong Kong Scanner Craft Company Ltd.
Printed and bound in Hong Kong by Leefung-Asco Printers, Ltd.

First Quill Edition
1 2 3 4 5 6 7 8 9 10

JACKET PHOTOGRAPHY by TONY CENICOLA STUDIO
and Judd Pilossof, Artemide, Paul Morin/Photo Trends,
John McDonough, McDonalds, New York Convention and
Visitors Bureau, Cindy Lewis Photography, NASA, William
Daley, Schenck & Schenck/Sam Maloof.

CATHERINE BUSH has written about contemporary live performance in publications ranging from New York's *East Village Eye* and the *L.A. Weekly* to *Spin* and *Vanity Fair.* She graduated from Yale University with a B.A. in Comparative Literature. In addition, she was the recipient of a Transatlantic Review Award for fiction.

ERIC FLAUM is a freelance writer and production editor at Time Inc. His articles have appeared in *The Chicago Sun Times, Esquire's Health and Fitness Clinic,* and a number of popular music publications, and he was formerly associate editor of *MGF* magazine. His father is a public high school principal and his wife is a teacher. Flaum lives in the New York City area.

ANDREA ISRAEL is a freelance writer who concentrates in food, travel, and television writing. Her articles have appeared in such publications as *The New York Times, Travel and Leisure, Signature, Vintage,* and *Family Circle.* She was formerly a script writer for "Search for Tomorrow" and is the author of *Taking Tea* (1987). She lives in New York City.

TERRI LONIER was trained as a studio artist and is currently executive director of the Empire State Crafts Alliance. She is also a consultant for the arts and business and has published numerous articles with *American Craft* magazine, *Fiber Arts, Metalsmith,* and *Metropolis,* as well as other publications. She is a frequent lecturer in the arts and business and taught for six years at various colleges in the West and Midwest. Lonier lives and works in New Paltz, New York.

JEAN MILLS is a freelance writer and editor. She is the author of *Babyworks: Every Parent's Sourcebook for Essential Baby Paraphernalia* (1985) and *Checkers: New Parents* (1985). She is currently in a M.F.A. program at City College in New York City. She lives in New York City.

ROBIN NAGLE is a freelance writer and editor and is currently a public relations representative for magazines in New York City. She lives in Brooklyn, New York.

KYLE RODERICK is an assistant editor at *US* magazine and a freelance writer specializing in fashion, beauty, and cultural reporting. She is the author of *Accessory Chic* (1986), *The Model's Handbook* (1985), and *The Complete Guide to Shaping Up* (1985). Roderick lives in New York City.

ALISON ROGERS is a freelance writer and reporter for *Adweek* magazine. Her beat covers advertising and promotional agencies in sports and the health and exercise fields. She was formerly a reporter for *Sport* magazine, and her articles also have appeared in *Sports Illustrated.*

SHARON SQUIBB is an artist living in Hoboken, New Jersey. She received her B.F.A. from the University of Tennessee, Knoxville, and her M.F.A. from the University of Cincinnati, where she taught drawing for two years. She has published a teaching journal for drawing with the University of Cincinnati (1983).

SUSAN S. SZENASY is the editor of *Metropolis: The Architecture and Design Magazine of New York.* She was formerly the editor of *Residential Interiors* and was senior editor at *Interiors* magazine. Her articles have appeared in *Connoisseur, Food and Wine, Home, Hotel and Restaurant Design,* and *Metropolis.* She is also the author of *Light: The Complete Handbook of Lighting Design* (1986), *The Home: Exciting New Designs for Today's Lifestyles* (1985), and *Private and Executive Offices* and *Office Furniture* (1984). She lives in New York City.

JOSEPH WALLACE is a freelance writer living in New York City. His articles on science, technology, and natural history have appeared in *Audubon, Sierra, Newsday,* and many other publications. Currently, he is working on a book about the latest deep sea exploration, one about the newest discoveries about dinosaurs, and a suspense novel.

ALL AMERICA

CONTENTS

ARCHITECTURE

Ezra Stoller © ESTO

High Museum of Art

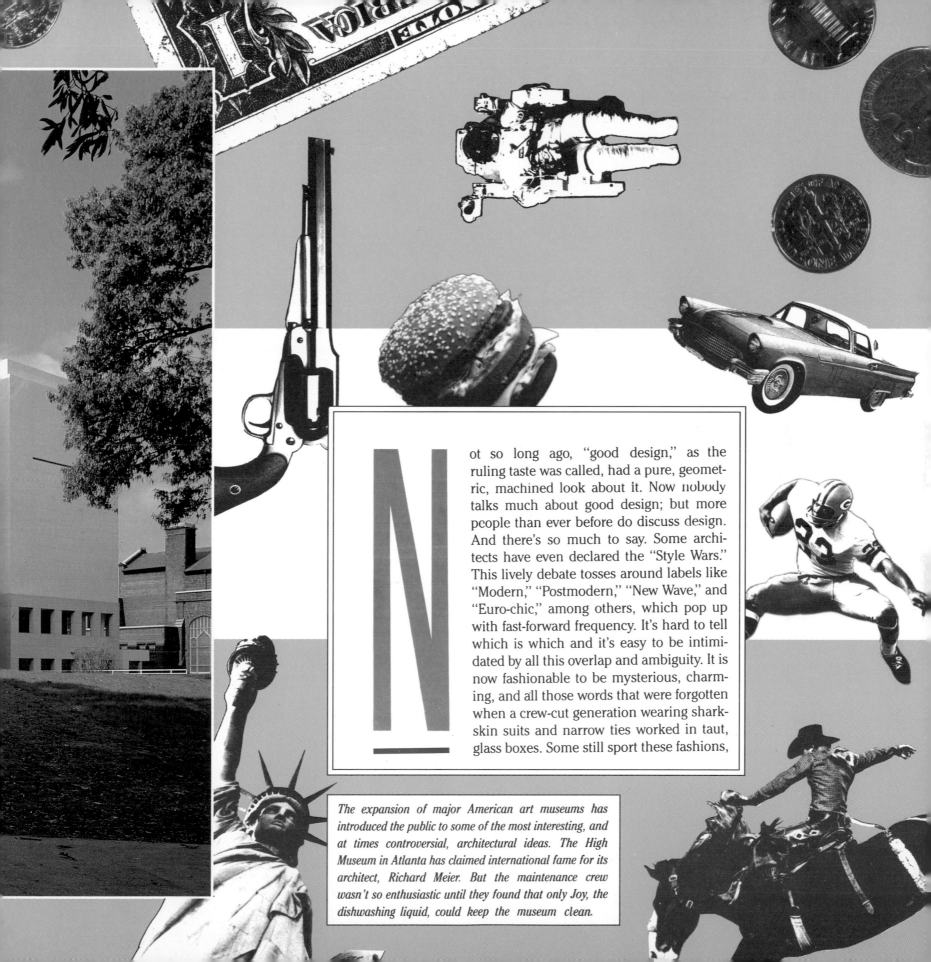

Not so long ago, "good design," as the ruling taste was called, had a pure, geometric, machined look about it. Now nobody talks much about good design; but more people than ever before do discuss design. And there's so much to say. Some architects have even declared the "Style Wars." This lively debate tosses around labels like "Modern," "Postmodern," "New Wave," and "Euro-chic," among others, which pop up with fast-forward frequency. It's hard to tell which is which and it's easy to be intimidated by all this overlap and ambiguity. It is now fashionable to be mysterious, charming, and all those words that were forgotten when a crew-cut generation wearing sharkskin suits and narrow ties worked in taut, glass boxes. Some still sport these fashions,

The expansion of major American art museums has introduced the public to some of the most interesting, and at times controversial, architectural ideas. The High Museum in Atlanta has claimed international fame for its architect, Richard Meier. But the maintenance crew wasn't so enthusiastic until they found that only Joy, the dishwashing liquid, could keep the museum clean.

but this time it's more by design than out of a fearful need to conform.

The turnabout from sameness to variety was predicted by the marketers of the 1970s. Their surveys revealed that people wanted more choice. The search was on, they said, for a connection with the historic, the ethnic, the regional, and the personal. The social and economic forces that brought about this change were signaling a new, more mature America.

The nation itself had celebrated its two-hundreth birthday and now had a history. The much-studied "baby boom" generation's spending power was increasing even as their metabolism was slowing down. As a result, it was foreseen that their larger, more public concerns were about to be redirected to personal accomplishment and gain. And finally, the realization came—briefly forgotten during the years of unrestricted expansion—that the earth's resources are finite and that the world is a fragile place. Architecture, the most visible and lasting of the art forms, was obliged to respond to these new values.

It began to make more sense to restore, renovate, and adapt old buildings—from grain elevators to churches—than to raze them. It became prudent to consider updating technologies designed for rapid obsolescence—such as systems of wiring, heating and cooling, and plumbing—and maintaining the things that were designed to last. The buildings that were saved this way revealed some extraordinary aesthetic surprises, many of which were forgotten or suppressed when the modern grid became dominant.

Restorers rediscovered irregular spaces, large and oddly shaped windows, rich materials and colors, and the workmanship that went into making these forgotten structures interesting. Their appeal was undeniable and the restoration of them revealed an abiding human need to seek out variety in decoration and spatial configuration. The offices architects chose for themselves were the most telling evidence of this new trend. Even as they designed cubist fantasies for their clients, architects' drafting rooms were often in great open spaces where tall, wood-beamed or pressed-tin ceilings were held up by fancy cast-iron columns. These products of industry, made before the machine achieved its lightning speed, took on the romantic allure of a more innocent time. And the high-ceilings and open spaces recalled the gracious atmosphere of rooms before they were compressed by the necessities of modern construction methods. The very things that made high-rise buildings livable—electricity and cooling technologies—took away hefty portions of ceiling space, which now contain the buildings' lifelines.

The new awareness of history had a much wider impact on architecture than merely validating the urge to save the old. It has changed the look of buildings. The declaration of this new freedom in design came, fittingly, from a young Philadelphia architect who was getting little work in the 1960s. Robert Venturi, now elevated to "father" of the so-called "postmodern" sensibility, challenged architects trained in straight-edged modernism to expand their repertoire of expression in his book *Complexities and Contradictions in Modern Architecture*. He called attention to the complex decorations and spaces builders had traditionally made to express the social, religious, and economic values and aspirations of the patrons who financed buildings.

Then, with his students and partners, Venturi began to study successful popular solutions to the problem of fast communication in a rapidly moving car-culture, which had become a fact of modern American life. The billboard, they discovered, had become more important than the building. This reality, they announced, held enormous significance to the way buildings respond to socio-economic forces. The idea, broadcast among architects who were used to designing subtle—often non-existing—signage to identify their glass-clad steel buildings, encountered some strong resistance at first. How could the blatant commercialism of the strip possibly be reconciled with the subtle aims of artists and architects?

That question is still in the process of being answered. Some have responded by combining popular expressions with the avant-garde, others by adding historical details to buildings' facades. So far, the solutions have tended to be only skin-deep, dressing the basic steel or wood skeleton in an attention-getting garb of marble, paint, metal or some array of new synthetic materials. These public-opinion teasers, structures that question, defy, or sometimes mock familiar architectural expression, are everywhere. In Wisconsin, a commercial strip is animated by an artful ruin built for the wares of a catalog retailer. On a Kentucky riverfront, an elegant neoclassical skyscraper announces the success of a new type of American enterprise: for-profit health care. In a Texas suburb, a cluster of expensive townhouses with colorful faces and jazzy bodies lure young urban professionals to neighborhoods where the single-family house is becoming an endangered species. On a California street, a rose window over a garage may signal the new freedom to ornament or identify the place as "The Shrine of the Holy Mercedes." And in upstate New York, a restrained, euclidian glass box—the well-known energy guzzler of recent memory—saves a chemical company's dollars with its ingenious sandwich of insulating, transparent skin.

And so, American architecture in the late twentieth century—the work of mostly

Tim Street-Porter

Robert Landau

Richard Payne

Americans live in more varied places than anyone could have dreamed about twenty years ago. Our influences come from that quintessentially American architect Frank Lloyd Wright whose many houses (like the one at top left) are being studied, renovated, and celebrated by the descendants of people who would have neglected such buildings a mere generation ago. Rambling Victorian homes, (like the exuberant specimen from the California Redlands, top right), provide many irregular, charming rooms that jut out into nature as belvederes, sleeping porches, balconies, and picture windows. The attempt to make multiple housing look like one great, expensive mansion is successfully achieved by the young Florida architecture firm of Arquitectonica in a Houston suburb, left, where each living unit has its own character while also being very much a part of the impressive complex.

Most people know about Humana Hospitals from watching the recipients of the artificial heart live their lives on television. But in the architecture community, Humana made big news when in 1985 its new building was completed in Louisville, Kentucky. Its architect, Michael Graves, who used classical elements to dress up a basic, steel-frame high-rise, was praised by critics for his ability to create a new American style: one that combines grandeur with public service. Even those who would have their architecture less decorated, admitted that the Humana Building established its patron firm, the for-profit-health-care-corporation, as an important, new force in American society.

Keith Glasgow

A new respect for American historical styles is shown by the careful preservation of turn-of-the-century and later buildings, even when these are surrounded by new, high-rise structures. In New York City, the Republic National Bank's old building, left, is gently embraced by the glass and steel structure that expands the bank's valuable floor space. In Los Angeles, known for its many fantasies, the Coca Cola Bottling Company building, below, was made to look like a grand ocean liner when those great floating structures plied the seas in streamlined, machined comfort that suggested an ease of movement and an always new horizon of technological and scientific conquests.

Robert Landau

Sandra Dos Passos

America's love affair with nature and the frontier manifests itself in buildings that rise on the rocky coast of Maine, right, *where the enclosed spaces offer a safe haven from the fickle elements of wind, sea, and earth. Some see these structures as intrusions into the greater scheme of things and want to keep our natural wonders just that, natural. Others see an opportunity to establish lucrative tourist businesses to serve a people always in search of the last frontier.*

native talent—is becoming more popular, if not more easily understood; more ready to appeal to the emotions, often to benefit builders who use design as a marketing tool; more prone to humorous one-liners and ambiguous comments; and more than ever interested in the cutting edge of modern technology.

It is technology, more than attractive decorations, that expresses the American tradition. In architecture, it was in the midwest, under the big skies of the prairie, that the two dominant building structures were developed that integrated modern technology with the need to house expanding businesses and gadget-oriented homes. Louis Sullivan's designs of tall urban buildings in the late nineteenth century integrated the steel skeleton with a decorative skin that expressed, in its upward soaring lines and proportions, the aspirations of a people on the rise. Sullivan's pupil, Frank

Lloyd Wright, designed the modern house with its mechanical core and open spaces that were organically connected with their natural surroundings. The ideas of these two quintessentially American architects were adopted by the European avant-garde during the early twentieth century. They gave a purity of design to the mechanically equipped building and brought this refined idea back to America when the turmoils of World War II forced radical artists and architects to seek refuge here.

It was no accident, then, that Ludwig Mies van der Rohe, the master of the transparent box, settled in Chicago and continued that city's great skyscraper tradition. Miesian purity, in fact, suited the rapid building techniques of the 1950s, when developers began filling cities with high-rise beehives and made the suburbs sprawl with Wrightean ranch houses. As a result, Americans became accustomed to hover-

ing floors, light-filled rooms, and machined air. In these artificial conditions, we somehow knew that the art and the heart were missing. Now the avant-garde is trying to get them back by making historical references to everything from Roman villas to Russian Constructivist stage sets.

Entertaining buildings, designed by Robert Venturi, Michael Graves, Philip Johnson, and a few others, call attention to the architect, who has become the superstar among design professionals. The accompanying publicity, which pinpoints the person responsible for the structure, also aids the growing need to discuss and understand an increasingly man-made environment. The public debate caused by unprecedented media attention on architects, their work, and the responses of people who use the built environment, is most forceful when the architecture touches emotions and challenges vague symbols.

Tony Cenicola Studios

The spirit of independent thinking, which is imbued in that humble structure of the American frontier, the log cabin, left. The cabin appeals to people eager to escape from the hyper-reality of urban life, yet who are unwilling to give up its conveniences. Instead, they are made cozy and warm by modern heating and lighting systems, and equip the cabin with a home computer that hooks into big-city data banks. The log cabin continues to represent old values while it's at ease with the new.

Featureless boxes for living, built during the great expansion of Southern California, are being made into individual dwelling places by residents with a sense of fun and fantasy. This Los Angeles bungalow, right, was enlivened by artist Peter Shire's addition of colorful sculptures and canopies of fiberglass, which accent the front door while protecting the entrance from the hot sun and the occasional rain.

Tim Street-Porter

Bo Parker

When the AT&T Building was finished in the early 1980s, it announced a new era in stylish high-rise architecture. The building's historic references to anything from Roman palazzos to Chippendale high-boys showed a new freedom of expression with decorative detail that came to be called Postmodernism. The style's most articulate advocate was Philip Johnson, the architect of New York's world famous AT&T headquarters, above. While decoration became the accepted expression of corporate America, purity of line and form (minimalism) an enduring expression of Modernism, caused some controversy in the building of the Vietnam War Memorial in Washington, D.C. Maya Lin, the architect who built the memorial, encountered the wrath of veterans for putting their war's memories into a hole in the ground.

Keith Glasgow

The event that best exemplifies the kind of debate architecture can induce concerns the erection of the Vietnam War Memorial in Washington, D.C. At first, no one was willing to call the structure a monument—a tough word that stands for a righteous cause. The memorial's apparent coldness wounded many veterans even though it was favorably received by many big-city architecture critics. Then the veterans and the public began to visit the place and trace their friends' names on the mournful black marble slab that reflected the viewers' own faces. What seemed, at first, to be just one more silent abstraction turned out to have content beyond its pure form. Its ambiguity and mystery, the often confusingly obscure qualities of so much design, worked this time to connect people to one another.

INTERIOR DESIGN

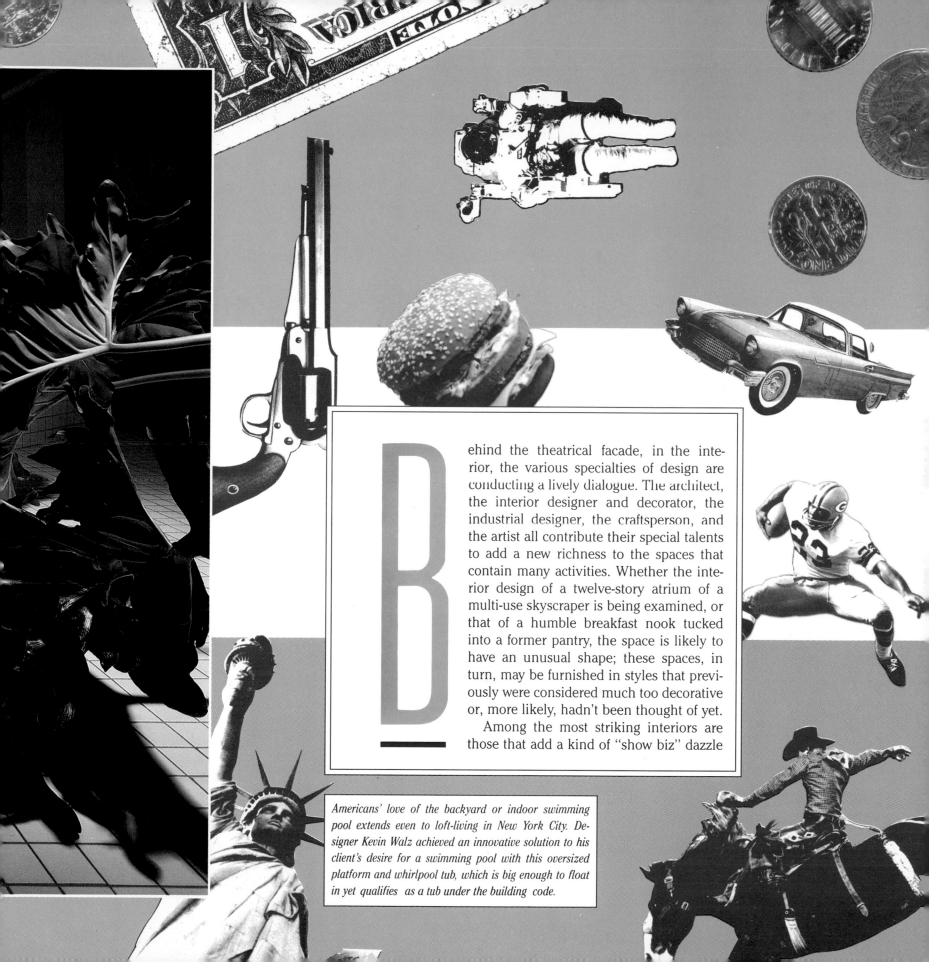

ehind the theatrical facade, in the interior, the various specialties of design are conducting a lively dialogue. The architect, the interior designer and decorator, the industrial designer, the craftsperson, and the artist all contribute their special talents to add a new richness to the spaces that contain many activities. Whether the interior design of a twelve-story atrium of a multi-use skyscraper is being examined, or that of a humble breakfast nook tucked into a former pantry, the space is likely to have an unusual shape; these spaces, in turn, may be furnished in styles that previously were considered much too decorative or, more likely, hadn't been thought of yet.

Among the most striking interiors are those that add a kind of "show biz" dazzle

Americans' love of the backyard or indoor swimming pool extends even to loft-living in New York City. Designer Kevin Walz achieved an innovative solution to his client's desire for a swimming pool with this oversized platform and whirlpool tub, which is big enough to float in yet qualifies as a tub under the building code.

Mark C. Darley

In New York City's reviving downtown where century-old industrial buildings are being converted to serve new needs, this lofty space with its old skylight was turned into the popular restaurant called America. Here the bar is the focal point of the large, open room where patrons come to watch each other, all wishing to be part of the "downtown social scene." In keeping with the American theme of the place, large abstract patterns that recall Indian sand paintings alternate with such imported images as misty paintings of the Statue of Liberty.

to even the most humble activities. Whether shopping or exercising, dining out or merely browsing in a museum, people today are likely to notice the design of the spaces that house these everyday events. The most memorable interiors are those that combine several experiences into one multimedia event. The interior has become a high style version of doing homework while watching TV.

The clothes shopper in Florida or New York, for example, is drawn inside the store Parachute by a grand procession of obliquely placed columns. This procession leads through a music-filled room where other people are strutting on metal catwalks and playacting in front of large mirrors while modeling the roomy pants and tops that resemble the garb of Samurai warriors and Shinto priests. Everyone on the floor seems to be competing with the fashion models who march to the rock beat of the videos that flicker on several screens.

Shoppers who care to pause notice that the clothes only *look* as if they were made of miles of fabric and that the hefty columns are, in reality, made of lightweight cardboard. It's all a show, a fabulous fake, an improvisational idea that is appealingly illustrated, many times over, in the pages of glossy magazines (which, by the way, are stacked on the rubber-tiled slabs that separate the industrial clothes racks). The electric sensibility energizes everything from viewers' hairstyles to the spot where they stand.

Because the young and the restless move hungrily from shop to restaurant to club, the owners of these places depend on designers to provide the stylish atmosphere that will keep customers coming back after opening night. A New York restaurant can compete with the hundreds of upcoming and established places only if it satisfies appetites that go beyond food: America does just that. This downtown bistro has

tables arranged in its large room so that everyone can see everyone. The huge bar is set deep inside the place to encourage the promenade of the well-dressed; an old-time skylight serves as a reminder of the city's architectural history; and the misty murals of familiar American images like the Statue of Liberty are overlaid with hard-edged Indian sand paintings. All of these design elements work to communicate the complicated culture that is America.

For those whose appetites for amusement have merely been teased during dinner, the art and video clubs are waiting. At some of these night clubs, the boundaries between art and life, fantasy and reality, as well as good and bad taste, are blurred. Here the interiors are changed as quickly as the listings of the top ten videos. This fast-forward metamorphosis is accomplished by artists in residence who explore, through material changes, leading edge ideas concerning space and enclosure, social indifference and involvement, cold and hot sexuality, and other modern preoccupations. Designed like live-in stages, the club interiors are disassembled quickly, then put back together as a new temporary set for living. In other clubs, the patrons experience even more ephemeral environments. They may be bombarded with video images—including their own—to the point of physical and emotional exhaustion. And so the instant interior and the interior of another dimension, until now hovering in some imaginary realm of science fiction, have become integral parts of urban life.

The same people who seek such sensual stimulation in their public lives often choose to retreat to quiet apartments and suburban houses cushioned, perhaps, with bucolic wallpapers and English chintzes. The brisk sales of these and other traditional furnishings seem to say that the home remains a refuge, a place where a

In New York, as in many metropolitan areas, a clothing store called Parachute, left, entertains young men and women with a barrage of fashion videos, a free-flowing interior architecture that encourages prancing in front of mirrored walls, and a display of many design-related magazines from Milan to Tokyo. In Texas, below, the mood is more subdued but equally innovative. The sculptural display counters have the powerful presence of great constructivist boulders. A watery light filters into this men's store through the dividing wall, which is made of glass tubes.

© Wolfgang Hoyt/ESTO

Wolfgang Hoyt/Esto Photographics Inc.

Thin layers of applied pattern revive some old systems of adding decoration to plane surfaces. The bent-ply chair by architect Robert Venturi, below left, has a screen-printed design. In a California bedroom, below right, adjacent to the obligatory outdoor hot tub, the walls are decorated with a frieze of stenciled patterns by architect Charles Jencks.

preindustrial dream is safely captured and maintained. But the dream of a simpler life is a mere surface decoration. It hides the high-tech machinery of the home where comfort is defined by computerized coffee pots and video cassette recorders which click on discreetly in the night.

In addition to being the container of electronic gadgetry, home is the place to make a knowing statement about the "hot" topic of design. It's where the man of the moment can show off his collection of furniture from the 1950s or his wildly colorful and nervous-looking chairs and lamps, which are aesthetic heirs of the era of "planned obsolescence."

Home is also the place to find comfort and relaxation. Unlike their predecessors, who tended to sacrifice the offending piece of furniture for a "unified style statement," the new designer integrates the old with the new. And so the clunky La-Z-Boy re-cliner is reupholstered in a fashionable fabric rather than discarded to make room for new furnishings.

In the material world of interior design, the most dramatic signs of change and of a new freedom of expression are the materials themselves. The same person who chooses a handcrafted desk made of rare woods and precious stones, for example, may be equally at ease with metal-mesh walls and silk upholstery that reflects light like an oil slick shimmering in a parking lot. The use of unexpected materials has a long tradition in American design that, at its very core, is highly experimental and adventurous. The most daring of all material explorers was Frank Lloyd Wright. He was known for giving his willing clients anything from patterned concrete to glass tube walls. Such materials are showing up in new, sleek incarnations, as the work of Wright and other masters are studied.

Artemide

Tim Street-Porter

Searching for unusual materials in unexpected forms has become a popular pursuit. Bearing witness to this trend are the many well-attended museum shows that showcase decorative arts to an interested public. These shows, like the Whitney Museum of American Art's 1985 "High Styles" exhibit in New York City, are accompanied by lush, elegant catalogs that explain the historical contexts of design expressions. In addition, many of the pieces on display in the museums are of recent design. Such new products benefit from the museum's stamp of approval. Because of this and because an adoring press shows the work of designers in gorgeous color photos, a large public is always anticipating the newest expressions from the studios of such architects as Robert Venturi, Michael Graves, and Frank Gehry. Design-conscious consumers seek out Venturi's cartoon-like, laminated wood "Chippen-

Corporations convey their enormous power by the interior spaces they claim for themselves. In the cavernous, marble-clad lobby of AT&T's New York City headquarters, designed by the architectural firm of Johnson Burgee, the only occupant of importance is a majestic, gold plated status, Genius of Electricity. "Golden Boy," as it came to be called, was made in 1914 for the top of the old American Telephone and Telegraph Company buildings by sculptor Evelyn Beatrice Longman.

Bo Parker

Being part of nature is just another illusion in the glass enclosed dining room of New York's Tavern on the Green restaurant, which juts into the wilderness of Central Park. Here nature is strictly controlled. The air is conditioned and the light is given sparkle by the crystal chandelier in case the sun fails.

dale" chairs, which are screen-printed with various wallpaperlike patterns; or Graves' classically-inspired coffee service, which is made of silver-glazed aluminum and mock ivory; or Gehry's fish-and-snake lamps made from chips of plastic laminates. These new products tend to blur the familiar division between the artful and useful.

The work of inventive architects and designers has created a climate of new possibilities in the most conservative interior space: the office, where the most complex issues of interior design and planning are gathering and competing with high technology. In these mostly high-rise, steel-and-glass structures, designers must integrate the requirements for air, light, and power while grappling with the many newly-spawned styles. Some happy solutions are found in offices surrounded by insulating glass walls where glare is reduced by adjustable louvers and other fenestration, and sunlight is brought deep inside by skylights, clerestories, and interior glass walls. Here the choice of colors, like pastels that diffuse the light and add to the overall brightness, is an essential part of the design scheme, not merely an arbitrary whim of fashion.

Faith in scientific methods has also made the new comfort in the office a more

personal one. The chair, the most intimate piece of furniture we come in contact with in public, continues to reflect—in its size and covering—rank over requirement. But as a result of painstaking studies which explore in detail the shapes, sizes, and movements of the human body, the office chair is becoming a more personal piece of furniture. It can be easily adjusted to an individual's height, posture, and support needs. Yet such ergonomic designs only begin to confront some of the issues brewing in the office. As more people sit in front of rapid-response consoles that demand longer periods of concentration than the paper and the pen, designers face a new set of problems. The disturbing overhead light reflected inside the ubiquitous computer console has led to the use of adjustable lamps on desks and torcheres, which throw an indirect, soft light on the ceiling. The electronic office also requires that desks be placed to express the individual worker's involvement with the always changing machinery. Whereas the old office was planned to accommodate "paper flow," the new office designer is beginning to recognize that information communicated through electronic impulses is bringing changes that are altering the way we do the most simple things.

Jayme Odgers/April Greiman Inc.

The increasing use of computers is demanding that new attention be paid to the lighting as well as the placement of machines that function like nothing we've known. In this San Francisco home office, left, *the computer console is placed with its back to the window so that its screen's images won't be disrupted by harsh sunlight. Materials, too, are being reconsidered. Formica, formerly considered a utilitarian surfacing material for the mass market, became an elegant, high-style product when the manufacturer added fashionable colors to its line of laminates. The Formica showroom in Chicago,* below, *shows the decorative potential of the material.*

Courtesy of Formica Corp.

CHAPTER 3 ★ FASHION

Bob Murray

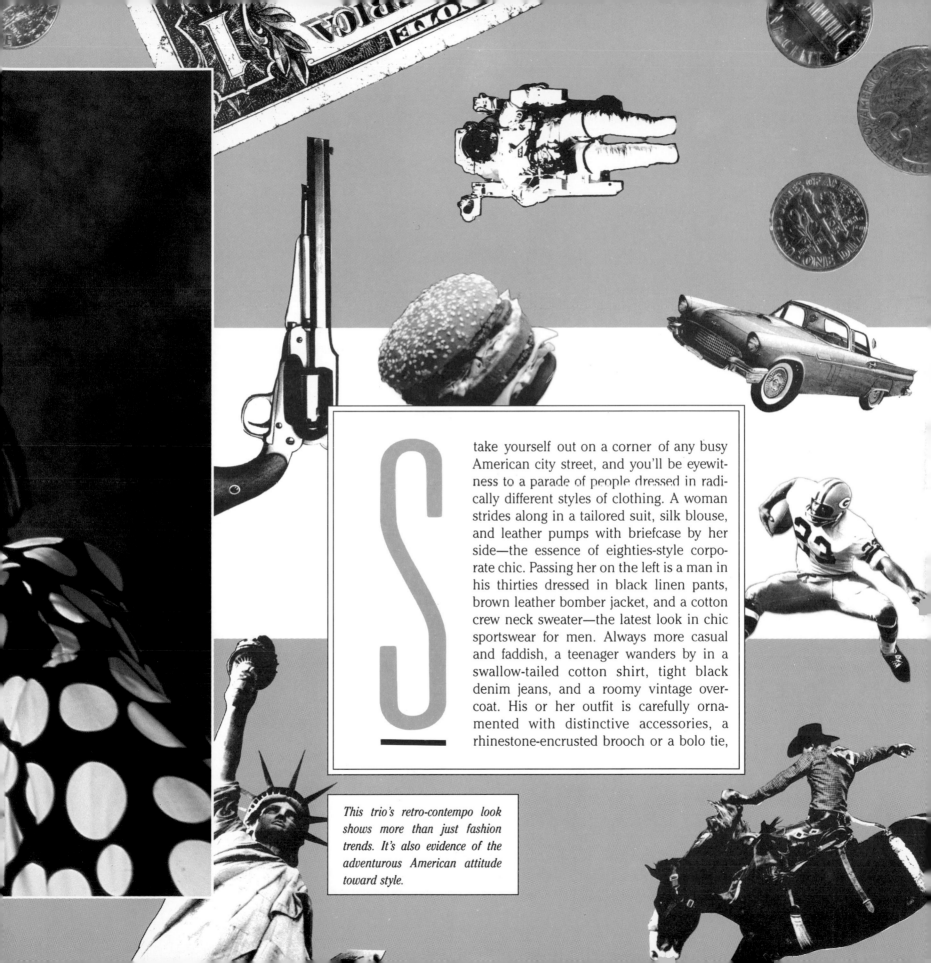

take yourself out on a corner of any busy American city street, and you'll be eyewitness to a parade of people dressed in radically different styles of clothing. A woman strides along in a tailored suit, silk blouse, and leather pumps with briefcase by her side—the essence of eighties-style corporate chic. Passing her on the left is a man in his thirties dressed in black linen pants, brown leather bomber jacket, and a cotton crew neck sweater—the latest look in chic sportswear for men. Always more casual and faddish, a teenager wanders by in a swallow-tailed cotton shirt, tight black denim jeans, and a roomy vintage overcoat. His or her outfit is carefully ornamented with distinctive accessories, a rhinestone-encrusted brooch or a bolo tie,

This trio's retro-contempo look shows more than just fashion trends. It's also evidence of the adventurous American attitude toward style.

Loren Hammer

Severe yet sexy, these forties-inspired suits and hats glamorize the female form while poking fun at traditional menswear. The look is punctuated with little girl anklets.

a lacy or cool scarf, black leather driving gloves, and high-top pastel-colored basketball shoes are noteworthy, though ephemeral, examples. Although these three ensembles are widely divergent in style and content, they each represent a distinctly pinpointed market in the American garment industry. Other popular segments of the U.S. fashion market are evening and formal wear, preteens, petites, active wear, lounge wear, and designer-label menswear and womenswear.

As in all cultures, American fashion is a language unto itself; most people choose their clothes and assemble their outfits to impress others. Other vital considerations are climate, professional environment, and a need for personal expression. While

bronzed, athletic Southern Californians garb themselves in revealing designer sportswear or go sockless 365 days a year, Midwesterners are much more constrained because of extremes in weather, as well as a cultural climate that frowns on office wear of half-buttoned Hawaiian shirts with faded Levi's. Moreover, concerning personal expression or relative "taste," a polyester leisure suit may be an appropriate ensemble for a prosperous Southwestern businessman, but to any image-conscious Bostonian or New Yorker, it is the ticket to East Coast social suicide.

Profound divisions in regional style and expectations aside, it is still possible to zero in on fashions that represent a distinctly American look. Fashion empires such as

those of Calvin Klein, Ralph Lauren, Norma Kamali, Liz Claiborne, and the late Perry Ellis deliver seasonal fashion statements that correspond to a vast range of lifestyles, taste levels, and bank accounts. In turn, their designs influence the character of more down-market collections, such as those put out by J.C. Penney or The Gap.

Though status-conscious Americans have acquired a more casual approach to dressing, they are just as loyal to their favorite designers as Europeans are to the masters of *haute couture*. A case in point is Calvin Klein, whose provocatively advertised designer jeans have been donned by everyone from high school kids to highbrow socialites. The success of Klein's jeans vaulted the rest of his collections to national prominence in department stores, where they continually dominate the non-Levis market. Klein's crisply tailored menswear and womenswear are noted for their impeccably updated classicism, while at the same time being stylish enough to be sexy.

Ralph Lauren, on the other hand, has built his international fashion empire by reinterpreting vintage and humble American clothing in fine fabrics at landed gentry prices. Lauren gets his inspiration from various indigenous styles of American dress. His most highly stylized and best-selling collections derive from heretofore un-chic garments. Some designs, for example, are powerfully popular expressions of all-American pioneer nostalgia: prairie skirts, high-necked, lacy blouses, and buckskin jackets. Others feature appropriated motifs from the Native American culture (which has already been co-opted by the social, political, and cultural powers that be). And, while his outdoorsy clothes glamorize the work ethic and rural, homespun values in America, his Polo line of sportswear, with its familiar polo-player

logo, projects a pseudoaristocratic, country-home image. What elevates Lauren above all other U.S. designers in any of these looks, however, is his genius for creating and marketing "visions of America" for Americans to wear. Ironically, those who can afford his romanticized pieces of national identity are mainly affluent urban professionals and suburbanites.

One designer who deliberately and successfully designs for the (female) masses is Liz Claiborne. Her clothing is made for women who work, hence it is affordably priced, and all pieces are coordinated with complementary accessories. Although her collections do not make revolutionary fashion statements, they are the most innovative of their kind because of their professional polish and distinctive use of color. Even more important, while more up-market womenswear designers continue to present skillful copies of male executive attire, Claiborne's garments dress women for success without the traditional elements of "corporate warrior" style. Yet another practical contribution Claiborne makes to American womenswear is her line of pe-

Perry Ellis Sportswear

The late Perry Ellis founded a fashion empire by designing for affluent but unpretentious Americans. This update on a classic all-American jacket, above right, *typifies his exuberant style. The lady in black,* right, *successfully mixes classic formal, funky, and street fashions.*

Bob Murray

Perry Ellis Sportswear

Perry Ellis's womenswear reveals as much as it conceals. With an approach that is classic and moderne at the same time, he creates witty clothing for a sophisticated audience.

tites clothing, which affords smaller-sized women the rare opportunity of dressing with authoritative panache.

In a more daring yet mainstream vein, trend-setting Norma Kamali's designs invariably dramatize the female in head-to-toe, *femme fatale* glory. Kamali is a "body-conscious" designer, and her work is instantly recognizable for its distinctive structural details. Boxy shoulder pads, campy ruffled skirts, and buttons as large as drink coasters mark her clothes with a tough but sexy seriousness. Depending on the attitude of the woman inside them, Kamali's clothes are worn as a celebration of femininity, a parody of female seductiveness, or as trashily alluring finery. American pop-culture icons haunt many Kamali designs, her couture ready-to-wear dresses are often reminiscent of costumes worn by film goddesses such as Joan Crawford or Lauren Bacall. Sci-fi film and comic book heroines also seem to influence the design of her exotically styled hats, coats, and belts.

Season after season, Kamali gives the fashion public something they never knew they wanted; she's the empress of highly synthesized style and content. Like Calvin Klein and his designer jeans, Kamali made a fortune from one innovative garment that ignited a raging fad; now classic fashion for both women and men, Kamali's down-filled "sleeping bag" coat continues to look chicly voluminous and utterly practical on all those who wear it. Her other master-works include luxuriantly draped and flamboyantly tapered dresses and separates made from sweatshirting material, gossamer-weight body stockings, and high-on-the-thigh swimsuits. To her dubious credit, Kamali also happens to be the first American fashion designer to enter the hair cosmetics field; her line of hair colors was introduced in the fall of 1986.

In marked contrast to the spirit of Norma

Kamali stands the menswear and womenswear of the late designer Perry Ellis. With exceedingly crisp craftsmanship, Ellis' expensive ready-to-wear and more casual sportswear collections exude youthful, upper-class gentility. And, while Kamali's clothes emphasize or exaggerate the physique of the wearer, Perry Ellis' trim, neat creations cover both sexes with establishment grace and fresh flair. His fashion approach won him numerous Coty awards (the fashion industry's highest accolade), for he achieved a marketable compromise between casual and sophisticated styling. Many of his most successful pieces are updated refinements of classic American garments. Ellis' cotton-and-wool knit sweaters, for instance, boast intricate stitching and handcrafted allure; his more elaborate sweater designs parallel tapestries in their detailed motifs. And, in the case of his sinuously tailored suits, jackets, and coats, Ellis' plush fabrics and subtle colors are standouts for their coherent styling and comfort. In the contemporary American fashion field, Ellis' designs represent the *ne plus ultra* of "post-preppy" clothing. Although Lauren, Klein, and Claiborne will continue to derive new looks from preppy styles, Ellis' creations will endure because they reflect considerably more imagination, wit, and skill.

No discussion of American fashion is complete without an exploration of its elusive yet influential origins. An appreciation of how regional styles and cross-cultural urban street looks cyclically blossom into national fashion trends is essential to an understanding of what Americans are wearing and why. The evolution of a clothing style's popularity often takes the following course: A certain segment of the population develops a defined and innovative style of dress and accessorizing. Designers take note of the style and reinterpret it for consumption by the mass market. Inevita-

The world's favorite rebel without a cause, James Dean, in the best of Western duds. Children's clothes today sport a surprising amount of sophistication, inset.

Bob Murray

bly, the detailed nuances of the original look get lost in the designers' mainstream translations.

Perhaps the most graphic example of a local look turned into a widely popular style involves the development of sweat clothes into a classic element of casual wear. The "sweat suit-ization" of America began in the mid-seventies, when fashion-forward blacks, Latinos, and other ethnic urbanites around the United States began wearing cotton sweatshirts, pants, and jackets with bold accessories, such as rhinestone jewelry, chiffon scarves, and high heels or leather high-top basketball shoes. This imaginative, low-budget "street couture" was further stylized by the wearer's artful scissoring of sweatshirt necklines, sleeves, and torso areas. Thus, these uniform exercise suits became highly personalized and often revealing glamour clothes. Dance students, incidentally, also began cutting and ripping their sweat suits to create more comfortable workout and lounging clothes. It wasn't until 1983, however, that this fashion achieved national exposure. In the blockbuster movie *Flashdance*, the teenage heroine wore shoulder-baring, ripped, gray cotton sweatshirts and nothing else but black stiletto high heels. Millions of Americans recreated the look they saw in *Flashdance*, either by cutting up their own clothes or by buying designer versions of sexy sweats. So goes the saga of an American fashion fad.

It should be noted that American fashion has always absorbed a substantial amount of its design ethos from English, European, Asian, and even Indian clothing styles. Yet between 1970 and 1980, the U.S. fashion industry clearly articulated a home-grown vocabulary of American clothing. The aforementioned "preppy fashion" is the shining example of authentic American gear. After the stylistic tumults of the 1960s, this rather bland wardrobe of the East Coast establishment elite has come out of the closet to achieve mainstream fashion status. This preparatory school or "Ivy League" style refers to natural-fiber, simply designed, and mostly unisex clothes and accessories. Legions of college students and prep schoolers have sported this seasonless, ageless look since the late

1940s. In fact, President John F. Kennedy was the first preppy to get major media coverage and so introduce this look to the national imagination. Look at photos of JFK romping on the beach at Hyannisport in the early sixties and you'll see the preppy wardrobe and the preppy aspirations of today, and always. With but a few postmodern embellishments (in style, but not in content), preppy fashion is a definite throwback, and therein lies much of its appeal. It reassures the wearer, in a sort of nostalgic and uniform way, that he or she is at the right school and on the right track to success.

Staple preppy garments include: Oxford cloth button-down shirts in blue, pink, yellow, or white; crew neck Shetland wool sweaters; baggy khaki or Breton red pants; corduroy or denim Levi's; Docksiders' leather moccasins; white leather bucks for dressing up in summer; Oxblood or black penny loafers for winter. Harris tweed jackets are *de rigeur* for both sexes. Female preppy fashion is identical to male in most respects. Where Chip wears a cotton navy turtleneck under his white Oxford cloth and green Shetland, Tracey is apt to combine a patterned turtleneck (tiny hearts, ladybugs, and anchors are popular motifs) with a monogrammed hot pink Shetland. She would complete her ensemble with a gold add-a-bead necklace, demure pearl stud earrings, an *Etienne Aigner* handbag, blue jeans, and pink canvas espadrilles.

Given that most people who dress preppy are striving for a special kind of societal success, the style's pervasive influence in designer collections, such as those of Perry Ellis, Calvin Klein, and Liz Claiborne, stamps it as a *bona fide* visual index of conservative cultural trends in America. Indeed, the runaway best-seller, *The Preppy Handbook*, wickedly spoofed prepster subcultural mores while it simultaneously popularized, glamorized, and legitimized

Bob Murray

Bob Murray

Bob Murray

them. Aspiring preppies and authentic ones alike studied essential wardrobe and attitude tips with all the zeal they brought to their college entrance exams.

So, although preppy fashion may have gained popularity through in-joke glamour, it ascended to core American-fashion status in the late 1970s and early 1980s. The sportswear and expensive leisure wear lines for men and women by designers such as Alexander Julian and Ralph Lauren (who, incidentally, once manned the tie counter at the quintessential preppy emporium, Brooks Brothers) have propelled the preppy's position to even higher heights. Furthermore, preppy style transmuted from trendy to the heart of the American fashion vocabulary when middle-class department stores like J.C. Penney and Sears introduced prep-gear clothing lines. Look at any major television commercial campaign, such as those of Burger King or Michelob, and see that everyone from a black teenager to a middle-aged career woman is sporting an Oxford cloth shirt, a rugby shirt, penny loafers, and a tweed jacket. Preppy regalia is here to stay: Long live the old school of presynthetic, postwar, forever-young fashion!

Another vital cause-and-effect relationship influencing American fashion exists between pop culture's media icons and the audience. Rock stars such as Bruce Springsteen, Tina Turner, and Madonna have made MTV a veritable twenty-four hour fashion show of sartorial inspiration or, as often is the case, outright copying by the viewers. Television stars such as Joan Collins of "Dynasty" effectively advertise opulent women's clothing. In fact, in a marketing stroke of life imitating art, an authorized line of "Dynasty" clothing was established. The top-rated TV series "Miami Vice" has raised male Americans' fashion consciousness to staggeringly stylish heights; Don Johnson, the star of the show,

Annie Leibovitz

NBC Photo by Frank Carroll

Rock 'n roller Bruce Springsteen and TV idols Don Johnson and Phillip Michael Thomas are three fashionable media icons who inspire the look of millions of American men.

is rarely on screen in anything less than three thousand dollars' worth of minimally tailored suits, chic cotton T-shirts, or tight, faded-just-right Levi's. Additionally, Johnson's shoes are often low-cut, Euro-style loafers in tropical, pastel colors. His aura is all the more dapper because he wears them without socks, a now widely imitated, ankle-baring look for both men and women.

Enough talk about the establishment designers and media-induced fashion trends that dictate who wears what and why and when. America is also full of vanguard designers who are creating some of the most aesthetically original and timeless clothing in the world. One such visionary is New York's Keni Valenti. Out of his black-and-gold-painted East Village boutique comes collection after collection of minimal dresses, suits, and separates that forge the missing links between modern sixties fashions and the twenty-first century. Without zippers, buttons, or any conventional detail, Valenti's richly hued, quasimonastic, and coolly flattering designs command a loyal following. His affordable prices make him one of the most accessible high-fashion designers in the country. Using only the richest fabrics (velvets, silks, 100 percent cottons, and linens), Valenti augments his collections with dramatically scaled accessories. He designs oversized, formal black-and-white straw hats, vests made of drapery rings, and chrome-and-brass bracelets fashioned out of car parts and household utensils. Several of the accessories he designed for New Wave clothing designer Betsey Johnson's line have been acquired by the New York Metropolitan Museum of Art's permanent collection. The international fashion press regularly features Valenti's work. *Women's Wear Daily, Harper's Bazaar, Time,* the Italian *Vogue* and *Elle* have all featured Valenti's designs.

Valenti credits his mother, a former go-go dancer on the "Hullabuloo" TV show of the sixties, as his primary fashion influence. "Every kid should have a mother with a twenty-inch waist and a new hair color every day. Although I design with the idea that less-is-more, I'm fascinated by street clothes, vintage couture by designers like Charles James, sixties space-age styles by Courreges, and all the crazy outfits that my mother wore, plus Barbie doll clothes."

Valenti's collections in lightweight crushed velvet, blue denim, and sweatshirt material create perfectly poised silhouettes on anyone from a twenty-five-year-old man-about-downtown to a style-conscious, middle-aged woman. The unisex and age-less style of Valenti's designs communicate a look that is ahead of the times and is also the shape of things to come.

Like Keni Valenti, fellow American designer Michael Kors believes that clothing must be adaptable to its wearer's personal style. But whereas Valenti creates fashion for twenty-first-century people, Kors designs for the traditionally chic, high-salaried woman whose life requires practically tailored turnouts. His clothes are distinguished by their rich tones and textures and pared-down, traditional shapes. For instance, he shows sleeveless turtleneck dresses, voluminous rayon broadcloth shirts over tight cotton-knit leggings, and scooped-back tank tops with black silk charmeuse boxer shorts. As Kors puts it so well, his garments are "beyond sportswear." His collections do indeed transcend the creations of any American designer working in this particular idiom and price range. Kors' creations possess a distilled elegance that is so relaxed and versatile that by adding or subtracting pieces at will, the wearer can look unassumingly casual one moment, black-tie sophisticated another, and maturely stylish, high-powered, and professional in the next. All of his garments are designed with self-assurance and restraint. Even Kors' details, such as a tiny handkerchief peeking out of a linen tunic, are the height of reserved grace. It is details like these, however, that make his, as well as Keni Valenti's, work the most engaging in American fashion. Whether they become part of the establishment led by Klein, Lauren, and Kamali is irrelevant, they've already made substantial contributions to the American silhouette.

Frank Maresca

This Michael Kors's turnout creates a sinuous silhouette with classic yet futuristic style.

Richard Litt

Frank Maresca

Barbara Rosen

ALL-AMERICAN FASHION CLASSICS

Archetypal all-American fashions are born out of clothes and accessories that somehow transcend gender, age, social status, and ethnicity. Here is an overview of nationally popular fashion classics. Regional favorites are also indicated.

SHIRTS:

Plaid or checked cotton flannel shirts; chamois and khaki shirts; cotton T-shirts with all kinds of slogans, logos, and college names; and sweatshirts with logos and names are all American classics. Vintage bowling and Hawaiian print shirts are popular in most urban areas, and contemporary versions of the same can be spotted across the country. Preppy Oxford cloth button-down shirts will always be an element of standard American garb, but they are not always neatly tucked and buttoned; shirt tails flapping in the wind seems to be just as acceptable.

JACKETS:

Apart from the denim jacket, cotton zip-front windbreakers and black leather motorcycle jackets are eternal American classics. In preppy circles, especially on the East Coast, tweed three-button jackets are worn by all ages and sexes.

SKIRTS:

In the Southwest, tiered and ruffled skirts in Navaho colors like deep purple and turquoise are classic. Denim miniskirts are seen across the nation on women of all ages. Wool, plaid, kiltish-type skirts in various lengths are enduring favorites in the Midwest. Middle- and upper-class Californians and Hawaiians wear tennis skirts year round. Sophisticates around the nation wear black leather skirts; miniskirts are especially classic.

New York designer Keni Valenti's red tunic, lower left, *is the shape of things to come in American fashion. Michael Kors's elegant bolero jacket,* left, *displays his genius for designing interchangeable separates. Both designers are inspired by everyone from Liberace to Cher to all-American country girls.*

BLUE JEANS:

Blue jeans and other denim pieces deserve a category all their own. They have been a staple of American style since they were invented. Though they are now a standard fashion element around the world (with Russian teenagers trading dearly for them on the black market), America will always be credited for the development of the enduring blue jeans.

Levi's, Lee, and Wrangler are the most classic and popular brands. A number of designers, such as Calvin Klein, Ralph Lauren, Gloria Vanderbilt, and Liz Claiborne, offer their versions of the classic styles, with snazzy stitching on the pockets and tapered legs.

Jeans are paired with any kind of shirt or top and with a wide variety of footwear, from tennis shoes to high heels or boots. In the Southwest, West, and various rural areas, cowboy boots are the *only* shoes to wear with jeans.

SHOES:

Running shoes, high-top basketball shoes by Converse or Pro-Keds, leather wrestling shoes, tennis shoes—these are all popular among teenagers and are fast becoming classics for people of all ages. Penny loafers, fifties-style high heels, riding boots, and motorcycle boots are also footwear classics. Eternally practical, American professional women on the way to work are often seen sporting tennis shoes, with dress shoes in a bag dangling from their arm.

ASSORTED ACCESSORIES:

Navy or red Western-style bandanas; baseball caps; Ray Ban Wayfarer or aviator sunglasses; thick white athletic socks; lacy scarves and hairbows; terry cloth headbands and wristlets for jocks in warm climates; surf trunks year-round for select Californians and Hawaiians—these are just a few of the more enduring classic American accessories.

John Deane

CONTEMPORARY CRAFTS

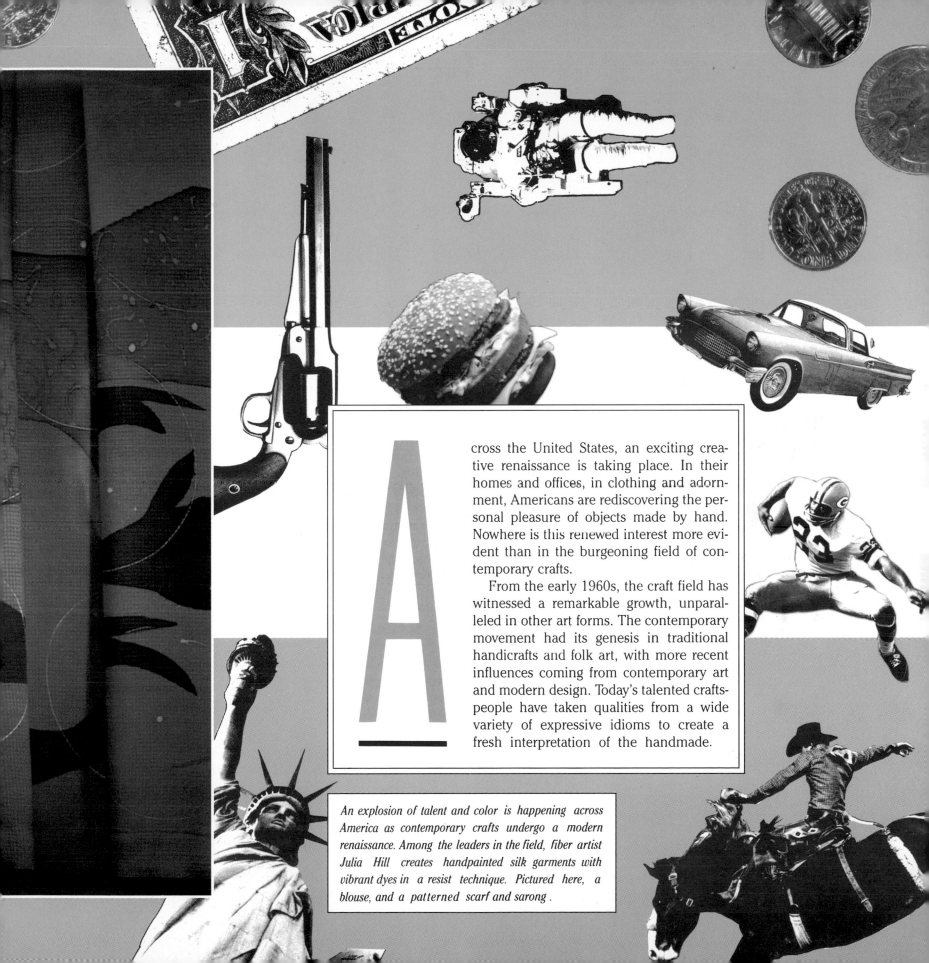

A cross the United States, an exciting creative renaissance is taking place. In their homes and offices, in clothing and adornment, Americans are rediscovering the personal pleasure of objects made by hand. Nowhere is this renewed interest more evident than in the burgeoning field of contemporary crafts.

From the early 1960s, the craft field has witnessed a remarkable growth, unparalleled in other art forms. The contemporary movement had its genesis in traditional handicrafts and folk art, with more recent influences coming from contemporary art and modern design. Today's talented craftspeople have taken qualities from a wide variety of expressive idioms to create a fresh interpretation of the handmade.

An explosion of talent and color is happening across America as contemporary crafts undergo a modern renaissance. Among the leaders in the field, fiber artist Julia Hill creates handpainted silk garments with vibrant dyes in a resist technique. Pictured here, a blouse, and a patterned scarf and sarong.

Diane Itter

Paul Avis/Mark Lindquist

In "Quilt Quartet," above, *Diane Itter creates a colorful miniature fiber painting (17" x 9") from thousands of tiny knotted linen threads. Second-generation woodturner Mark Lindquist often studies a tree limb or log for years to discover the form "hidden" inside and what shape the piece will become,* left.

Contemporary craftspeople link America's past and present. Crafts have played a vital role in the nation since its earliest beginnings, from the era of Paul Revere's silversmithing and other colonial enterprises. Through the years, crafts have been an integral part of American life, passing a legacy of skill and cultural meaning from one generation to the next. Today, most contemporary crafts are created in one of five traditional media: clay, fiber, glass, metal, or wood.

While today's artisans use materials and methods of time-honored tradition, the objects they create reflect a sensibility and aesthetic of the modern era. Contemporary crafts range from well-designed functional objects used in daily life to pieces that are on the leading edge of aesthetic exploration. In material as well as meaning, these works capture the spirit of the past infused with a sense of the present, invigorating traditional craft with contemporary aesthetics and techniques.

Craft items are as diverse as the artists who create them. From traditional to contemporary, functional to decorative, the spectrum of contemporary crafts displays the imagination and variety of its makers. All across America, in small towns and major urban areas, independent craftspeople are at work, creating ceramic dinnerware, glass stemware, one-of-a-kind art wearables, wooden tables and chairs, jewelry incorporating precious and nonprecious materials, and other craft art.

Contemporary crafts bring an intimacy to life that comes from objects made by hand. These works reaffirm the human spirit in an age of advancing technology and alienation. There is simple dignity in a handcrafted bowl or a woven shawl, and a silent union between maker and owner. This personal quality is, perhaps, the craft object's greatest appeal. Crafts today can be found integrated into nearly every area of modern life, from a handworked desk commissioned for an executive office to a set of picnic flatware in brilliant hues. The field is diverse enough to offer quality pieces for nearly every budget, from a few dollars for a ceramic mug to several thousand dollars for a major work of glass art.

The aesthetic quality found in today's fine crafts is leading them to be displayed more frequently in galleries and museums. Many specialty design areas of major department stores now carry fine crafts as well. Buyers can also purchase works—or place special orders—direct from the private studios of the craftspeople themselves.

For a better understanding of contemporary crafts, one can think of the works in three broad categories: crafts for use, crafts for personal adornment, and crafts as expressive statement. Of course, the classification of individual pieces usually overlaps into at least two of the three categories, for the maker's expressive statement is indigenous to any handcrafted piece. Furthermore, while some pieces may be created primarily as expressive statements, many are inspired by some functional origin springing from the history and tradition of the medium. An examination of each of these categories and how they overlap is helpful in gaining an understanding and appreciation of crafts today.

T. Buechner

Schenck & Schenck/Sam Maloof

The sweeping contours of Sam Maloof's handcrafted rockers display the masterful union of form and function. Prized for their beauty, comfort, and quality, the chairs are in such demand that Maloof has back orders for nearly a decade. Randall Darwall's handwoven silk scarves, right, *are products of the artist's skill and serendipity at the loom. The artist designs while weaving, letting the colorful threads and rich textures inspire each unique piece.*

Randall Darwall

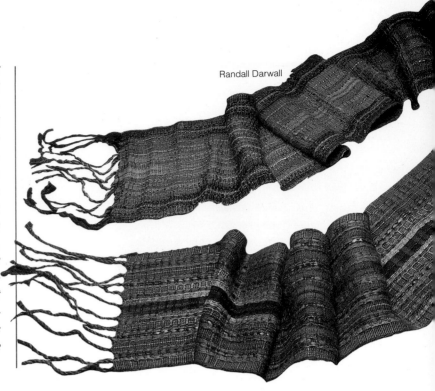

CRAFTS FOR USE

Ever since simple crockery and woven coverlets were crafted for use during colonial times, crafts have been an integral part of American homes. In today's era of mass production and stylistic uniformity, handcrafted functional items have widespread appeal. For many, the ritual pleasures of preparing food and dining are enhanced when accompanied by special utensils and tableware made by hand.

Wheel-thrown porcelain or stoneware dinnerware reveals the sensuous mark of the potter, with each unique piece belonging to a "family" of related forms of plate, cup, saucer, and bowl. Hand-blown glass stemware gives a sense of occasion to any wine, and even berries become a celebration when brought to table in a basket of glass or clay. Handmade knives show an awareness of materials, balance, and craftsmanship that make them a joy to use on a daily basis.

Color plays a prominent role in contemporary craft design, as artists use technology to go beyond the earthy tones of traditional craft materials. Brilliant hues are found in the most unexpected places—like David Tisdale's aluminum flatware. Tisdale has experimented with a process of anodizing this common metal, creating a remarkable palette of bright pink, azure, mustard, and teal. Equally colorful, but in more subdued tones, are the dyed reed baskets of Kari Lonning. With their woven graphic designs and subtle shadings, these baskets bring individuality to any room, whether sitting empty or gently brimming with a bunch of flowers.

Many artists working in clay and glass have created a similar explosion of color in their work, using defined bands and patterns of pure color in harmony with striking silhouettes. These vases and bowls—often rendered in a post-modern palette—enhance modern living spaces with their color and style, and bring a personalized touch to modern interiors.

Contemporary fiber artists have also interpreted craft tradition with modern designs and styles. Frequently, quilts, rugs, and other flat works in fiber are woven in bright splashes of color and pattern. Today's quilters may be found at high-tech sewing machines, using fabrics specially dyed or manufactured for their work. Many of these craftspeople are painting with fabric, using bright blocks of color to create new patterns or adapt traditional ones. Today's fiberworks—like their historic counterparts—continue to give both physical and spiritual comfort to their owners.

The richness of wood has attracted craftspeople for hundreds of years. While some modern artisans create furniture resembling traditional pieces, most contemporary craftspeople are developing new forms and designs. Influences from design groups such as Memphis can be seen, but most contemporary furniture artists bring their own personal vision to the field, an aesthetic that evolves from a true understanding and mastery of the medium. This is in contrast to a designer's approach, which often emanates from concept and drawing on paper and is later translated to an appropriate material.

For example, master woodworker Sam Maloof has spent more than thirty years

Josh Simpson

These cobalt goblets by Josh Simpson are completely hand-blown, using no forming molds. Employing traditional tools and techniques, the artist masterfully matches one glass to another by eye. The result is a group in which each glass retains an individuality and human element while remaining part of a set.

creating furniture. His rocking chairs demonstrate the special union of craftsman, material, and idea. Maloof's chairs are in such demand that he has a waiting list for orders for the next seven years, at prices of several thousand dollars each. The artist's sensitivity to materials and his attention to detail make his chairs not only comfortable but also a visual delight.

In contrast to Sam Maloof's serene rockers, several contemporary furniture makers have blended a sense of whimsy and humor in their works. Desks for executive offices have hidden drawers and flashing lights. The arms, backs, and legs of tables and couches are wood pieces carved into the shapes of playfully exotic animals. Tripod legs of end tables are curved and brightly painted, as if the piece might come alive to wiggle and dance. Furniture artists who create these works have all been trained in traditional woodworking techniques to create pieces of structural integrity, yet each adds his or her artistic personality to the work. This mastery of skill matched with a unique aesthetic style is a hallmark of the finest contemporary crafts.

Color plays a prominent role in contemporary crafts. In these aluminum butter knives, designer David Tisdale has adapted an industrial technique of anodizing the metal to create a fresh and colorful approach to flatware.

David Tisdale

Susan Hubbard Hamlet

Susan Hamlet is one of a growing number of contemporary jewelers who are looking beyond traditional precious materials to the common discards of our modern environment for inspiration in their wearable works of art. In her "Shin Bracelet #9," above, the artist has combined stainless steel, sterling silver, plastic, and pearl.

CRAFTS FOR PERSONAL ADORNMENT

Two of the most exciting areas in contemporary crafts are wearables and contemporary jewelry. Both are expanding the notion of what craft can be, as artists experiment with materials and forms that ultimately merge with the fields of fashion and art. Some wearables and contemporary jewelry also enjoy an intriguing artistic duality: when not being worn, many times they are hung or displayed as aesthetic objects.

Art wearables encompass creative clothing that ranges from masterfully woven scarves to luscious hand-painted silk garments and shawls. Many textile artists delight in exploring the range of color and pattern they can create within the perpendicular context of traditional warp and weft. Technological innovations abound, from newly discovered dyes to computer-aided designs that expand the possibilities of the woven grid.

Other craftsmen find the kimono shape appropriate for their artistic experiments. Simple in form and construction, it allows for relatively flat areas to be worked like a painter's canvas. Artist Tim Harding pushes this concept of clothing and construction to new frontiers. Bringing a painter's sensibility to his work, Harding adds an ironic twist to his colorful coats of layered cotton. To create the geometric patterns of the garment's design, the artist must cut deep diagonal slashes into the fabric, revealing the colorful interior layers and textures. His unusual technique—which would be considered destructive in most media—results in tactile, wearable works that delight the mind and the senses. Splayed flat on a wall, Harding's coats become vibrant textile paintings.

Master jewelers working today in gold, silver, and precious stones continue to create one-of-a-kind works of beauty that have pleased wearers through the centuries. These craftspeople continue the long tradition of fine European jewelry making, working within the self-imposed restrictions of the most expensive materials and painstaking techniques. Their joy may come from an innovative setting of a stone or the pleasure of matching the quality of their craftsmanship with the fineness of their materials.

It is in the jewelry of nonprecious materials, however, that one can see the creative vitality of the contemporary crafts movement. Faced with rising gold prices in the early 1980s, and seeking a fresh approach to creative expression, younger artists turned to common, cast-off materials and the unpretentious discards from daily surroundings for inspiration and materials. Plastics, rubber, paper, and stone combine with superior craftsmanship to produce startlingly inventive jewelry. Slivers of slate or rusty nails are juxtaposed with fourteen-karat gold in Pat Flynn's palm-size brooches, while Roberta Williamson carves whimsical drawings in her ivory scrimshaw. Like most art, the value of these pieces lies beyond the inherent worth of their simple materials.

Such works have revitalized jewelry as an art form by fostering its appreciation as ornament as well as miniature sculpture. Arline Fisch employs textile techniques of machine knitting to transform coated copper wire into striking neck collars and bracelets of bold color and design. Other jewelry artists use architectural elements that speak about space, line, and dimension as well as fashion and design in their wearable bracelets. The intimate scale of much contemporary jewelry enables it to be appreciated on the most private level.

William Daley

K. Staubitz/C. Thiesen

With startling innovation, Tim Harding slashes through multiple stitched layers of dyed cotton to create the textured patterns of his limited edition coats. Through careful dyeing and cutting, the artist has created an expansive landscape in "Sea Level," left. When not worn, the coats are often displayed as tactile paintings. Ceramic artist William Daley explores the geometry of interior and exterior shapes in his stoneware vessels. "Shang Play" (17" high x 25" diameter), above, is from the corporate collection of US News & World Report.

CRAFTS AS EXPRESSIVE STATEMENT

The love of a craftsman's material— whether clay, glass, fiber, metal, or wood—is central to his or her work. An illustration of the quest for this passion is the comment by woodworker Mark Lindquist that he will live with a piece of wood, often for a year or longer, before he fully understands what form the tree limb holds inside and what it may become.

Many contemporary crafts are works created primarily for personal expression, as an artistic exploration of the medium or form used. While these works may be inspired by functional uses—and in some cases may actually be adapted to a utilitarian end—the maker's intention is principally aesthetic.

Some sculptural works are artistic explorations of the vessel form, a shape rich in meaning throughout history. From the earliest mud and grass baskets to Grecian urns and European crockery, the vessel has been a part of the continuum of civilization's development. Today craftspeople use the vessel's form, history, and meaning as inspiration for their work: The ceramic pieces of William Daley lead one to ponder the geometry of inside and outside surfaces; the delicate blown glass of Dale Chihuly calls to mind sea forms and of the fragility of all organic life. Today's basketmakers construct sculptural forms that remind one of our ancient heritage and of the modern world. Whether using traditional reeds and grasses or brightly colored plastics, the basketmaker's techniques remain fundamentally unchanged and united with craftspeople through the centuries.

Several contemporary craftspeople use figurative imagery in their works to create personal narratives. Similar in content to figurative painting, these works often come closest to making the distinction between contemporary craft and art an invisible

Many of today's craft artists work in conjunction with architects and interior designers on large-scale pieces for private homes or public sites. One of the country's leading blacksmiths, Albert Paley was commissioned to create a pair of architectural gates in steel, brass, and bronze for the New York State Capitol Senate Chamber in Albany, New York.

one. Artist Dan Dailey's flat glass tableaux feature cartooned figures that offer both witty and revealing insights into human interchange. Other artists use craft media to create autobiographical and figurative works—some through drawings on the surface of vessels, others by sculptural forming of the material itself. Each work captures the personality and presence of its maker.

The massive clocks meticulously fabricated by woodworker Wendell Castle also have a presence, and often a humorous one. Castle has given each of his towering sculptures a personality, frequently incorporating visual puns into his works. *Trompe l'oeil* is prominent in Castle's work, where he masterfully gives the illusion of incongruous elements, such as layers of draped fabric, executed in carved wood.

For these sculptural craftspeople, like others working to make objects for use or to wear, the challenge is to master both material and idea, uniting them to create an object of personal expression.

As more individuals become aware of the place for fine crafts in their lives, the field is flourishing. Whether designed for use in the home, as wearable art, or for sculptural expression, contemporary crafts encompass an exciting diversity of materials and styles that is expanding daily. From the massive wrought iron architectural gates of Albert Paley to the miniature thread paintings of Diane Itter, today's American craftspeople are creating lasting works that show a mastery of material and new avenues of meaningful personal expression. Like this nation's earlier artisans, their legacy is the object made of integrity and love, a meaningful and enduring part of daily life that is passed to the generations of tomorrow.

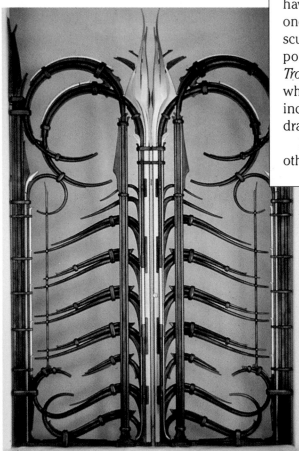

Albert Paley

Among the many contemporary craft artists who use figurative imagery in their work, Dan Dailey creates flat glass tableaux that present human encounters charged with satirical humor. In "The Critic," right, the artist's comments cannot be heard, since the critic has no ears. Dailey has incorporated vitrolite, brass, aluminum, and oil paint into the wall piece, measuring 36" x 48".

Dan Dailey

In our age of advancing technology, the allure of contemporary crafts lies in the pleasure of using simple objects which carry the human spirit of their makers. The understated elegance found in pieces such as these by glass artist Arthur Reed, right, conveys a timeless beauty that is cherished by those who collect and use contemporary crafts in their daily lives.

Arthur Reed

BUYING CONTEMPORARY CRAFTS

How does one determine the quality of contemporary crafts? Whether buying crafts at a gallery or museum, a department store or a crafts fair, several general characteristics are found in fine crafts. Consider the following when buying craft items.

1. *Mastery of material.* Does the artist understand the medium (clay, glass, fiber, wood, metal, etc.), and is the work well executed? For example, are the edges of ceramic mugs and glassware smooth to the touch and comfortable to use? Do woven works have even spacing of threads and finished edges? Joints in metal and wood should be clean and neat. Look for attention to detail and quality finishing.

2. *Truth to material.* A fine craft object should be matched to its appropriate material. Would you prefer a goblet made in glass, clay, or metal? Has the craftsperson chosen the best material to express his or her idea?

3. *Function.* Does the piece successfully fulfill its role as a functional object? Are the works enjoyable to use? Pitchers and teapots should not be too heavy when filled with water. Other kitchen items, like knives, should be properly balanced, and glass stemware should remain stable when full. Furniture must have sound structural design to support intended weight. Clothing should wear properly and have working closures and fasteners.

4. *Design and originality.* Is the piece pleasing to the eye in form, color, texture, and overall design? Does it mimic work already on the market, or is it an original approach? Is there a sense of individuality and personal style evident in the craftsperson's work?

FOOD AND DRINK

Tim Street-Porter

FOOD

Americans are having a culinary love affair that is connecting them with their folklore, history, diverse geography, and ethnicity. The so-called new American cuisine attempts to define this gastronomic melting pot. Some say there is no such thing as American food, while others say that American cuisine is a catchphrase coined by the media. Still, some swear that Cajun and creole cooking are the heart of American cuisine because they are indigenous to the United States. The same could be said of the New York City bagel or San Francisco's sourdough bread, though their roots can be traced to European traditions. The

Since its associations with 1950s America, the diner has been revived as the home of "mama," or home, cooking. From the roadside truck stop diner, to the more sophisticated urban revival, diners feature meat-and-potatoes cooking at its best.

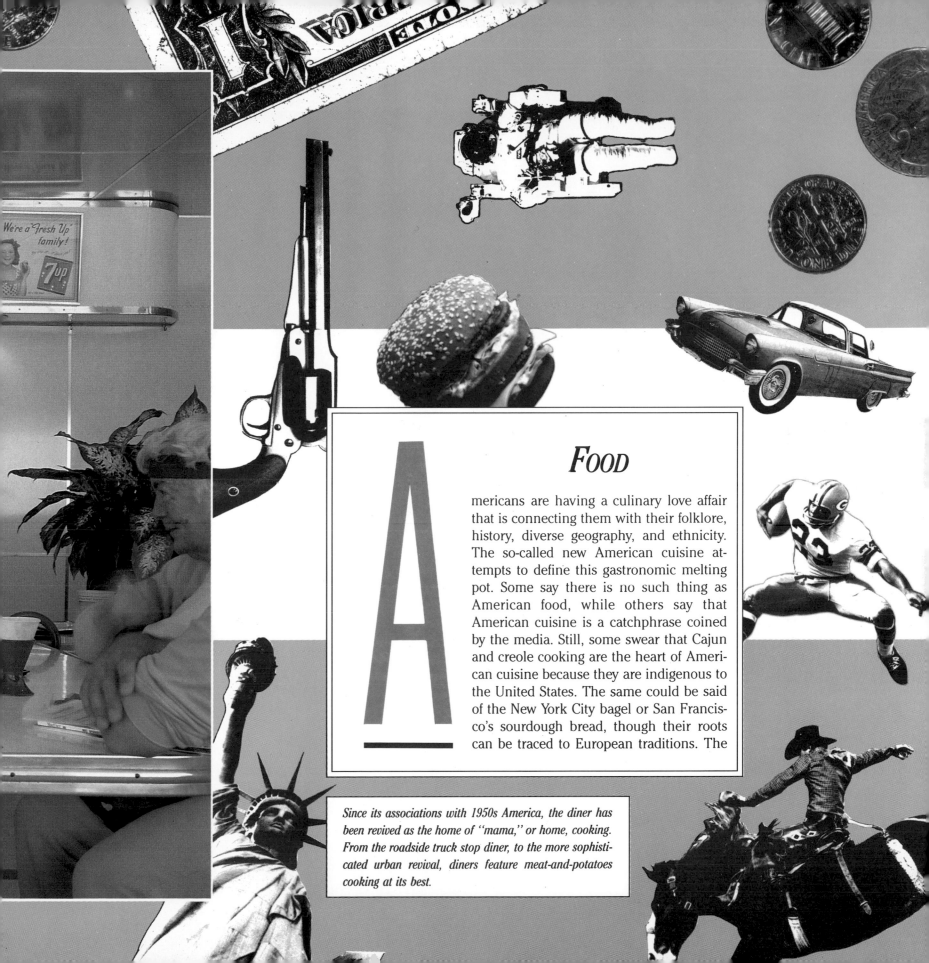

John Dominis/Wheeler Pictures

Judd Pilossof

Home cooking in America is as varied as the country is vast. The Dagwood sandwich, right, *a mountainous conglomeration of sliced meats, cheese, tomatoes, and whole-grain mustard is the hallmark of the diner, complete with a jukebox and stale coffee. In Hawaii,* above, *the pig roast is a standard culinary affair. It is buried in a pit and smoked. In the Deep South,* facing page, *okra, crawfish, vegetables, and spices combine with an African-Spanish-French influence to make rich gumbos and stews.*

trademark of the new American cuisine seems to be a marriage of cultures and trends—elements of classical French and Italian meet with Southern and Oriental. Healthful practices of low salt, fat, and cholesterol cooking abound while, at the same time, rich desserts are ever popular—perhaps rewarding those who abstain from alcohol or meats.

One of the biggest influences on American cooking was the nouvelle cuisine of France. It promoted the chef as celebrity and encouraged the use of indigenous and fresh ingredients as well as artistic presentation. As chefs tried to define their own styles, they drew upon regional heritage and indulged in a sometimes overzealous mixture of the unusual. A result of this experimentation with diverse foods is cuisine moderne, a blending of the classic and nouvelle that favors light and delicate ingredients combined with sharp flavor contrasts and shimmering colors. Restaurants offer foods that range from the exotic to staple American fare. Chèvre tarts, blue cornmeal tortillas, cilantro-spiced salads, wild mushrooms, miniature garden vegetables, free-range chickens, blackened redfish, fried orange squash blossoms, meat loaf, fried chicken, home fried potatoes, strawberry rhubarb pie, and even old-time peanut butter and jelly sandwiches are highlighted across the country, and sometimes found on the menu. The savvy diner looks for shape, color, variety, what's new, and what evokes memories. More than ever, food is an overall sensual experience.

REGIONAL CUISINES

Contributing to America's diverse cuisine are its distinct regional fares born of various ethnic backgrounds and geographic conditions. Spicy food, for example, which is borrowed from Hispanic and Oriental cuisines, is one of America's biggest taste sensations. With the likes of jalapeños and dried ginger in dishes like Texas chili and Szechuan chicken. Cajun and creole cooking, too, have taken hold of Americans' taste buds with jambalaya, barbecued shrimp, and boiled crawfish. While perishable products such as fish make Southwestern cuisine expensive, chilies, corn products, and beans have become associated with this cooking because they are more affordable. The Southwest's outgrowth, Tex-Mex, provides blue-corn tortillas with jalapeño peppers to be chased down by an icy-cold marguerita. California cuisine made its way east and set a standard for innovative combinations of fresh vegetables, fruits, and game. Spa cuisine was developed for the health conscious—it is low in

Jeff McNamara

Tim Street-Porter

fat, sodium, and sugar, with a premise that the visually exciting dish comprised of the freshest ingredients will satisfy the most deprived dieter. The Four Seasons restaurant and chef Michael Stroot of The Golden Door Spa were innovators in this field. The Northwest shares its indigenous love for fish like smoked salmon. New England's heritage is rich with seafood like lobster, scallops, and hearty sea chowders, as well as cranberries, baked potatoes, and the runner-up for title of National Bird—should the bald eagle decide to resign—the turkey.

Southern cuisine, which hails from the Florida Keys to Virginia, has exposed the rest of the nation to black-eyed peas, kale, mustard greens, sweet potatoes, pecans, strawberry and peach shortcakes, and key lime pie.

All of these regional influences have led to a down-home movement that is attributed to the baby-boomers' nostalgia fetish. "Mama" cooking revives American classics —from diner food such as the plate of pot roast and frowned-upon lumpy mashed potatoes to the grilled-cheese sandwich

Mother fixed for a quick lunch. The 1980s difference: Lumps in the potatoes are sentimentally preferable, and the sandwich is goat cheese grilled on five-grain bread.

THE RESTAURANT

The gastronomic tastes of Americans have dramatically changed since America became health conscious. Americans are consuming fewer calories and are more particular about what they eat. Single parents, two-job families, and a predominant class of young urban professionals don't have time to cook unless it's for a party—which is often catered. This generation of upwardly mobile baby boomers is the first one to have been brought up on restaurant food; and the restaurant is their source of entertainment and sociability—our new theater. Americans are eating casually—some call it grazing—partaking of a series of small snacks or dishes with an emphasis on lightness. Popular cuisines like Japanese sushi and Spanish tapas, for example, accommodate grazing habits. People are more willing to experiment with once unfamiliar produce like kiwi, spaghetti squash, sunchokes, mache, golden beets, purple lettuce, yellow peppers, and apple-pears. Clarity of presentation is preferable to food that is sculptured, disguised in sauces, or hidden by excessive herb mixtures.

Restaurants cater to America's "grazers," who are dining out in droves. Americans are spending more money on restaurants than ever before and on the average they eat out between three and four times a week. The restaurant scene is as varied in ambience and cuisine as the nation's tastes, but the common denominator is a rising and continued interest in healthy eating. Fish accounts for every three dollars spent, and restaurants are importing international fish as a result of improved refrig-

eration techniques. Informal grills, cafes, and brasseries are popping up in every state. The best seat in the house offers a view of the kitchen. Sushi and tapas bars, glass tandoori ovens, pasta makers in full view, at-the-table grills, and carry-out shops allow the customer to witness preparation. The chefs become performers, and their cooking is entertainment. Restaurants boast of pit fires fed by grapevine cuttings, hickory, fruitwoods, sassafras, and mesquite. Open-kitchen rotisseries cook meats, fish, and poultry, as unwanted fats drip into leaping flames. Wood-burning ovens provide a plethora of pizza for the upscale crowd—the familiar fast-food is turned into a contemporary gourmet dining experience with thin crusts, fontina, sun-dried tomatoes, and truffles. Pasta is served in every shape and color—boxed is out, homemade and hand-cut ravioli stuffed with spicy sausage in a chèvre cheese sauce is in. For dessert, well, some would say that's why Americans exercise so vigorously. The interest in health has not left the country devoid of a sweet tooth. Bourbon-whisky cake, brown Betty, and bread pudding rise from regional pasts. Home-baked is proudly displayed at restaurants serving the humble American apple pie or an exotic kiwi-persimmon tart.

The American diner, once the mainstay of the itinerant truck driver and other road food connoisseurs, has become the emblem of home cooking, or "mama" food. The Fog City Diner in San Francisco, far left, and The Empire Diner in New York City are two examples of the updated, revamped diner.

Tony Cenicola Studios

Nouvelle cuisine, right, emphasizes quality not quantity. Fresh vegetables, herbs, and a well-presented design of the food are nouvelle cuisine's ingredients. "Surf and turf," far right, is a slang term for the favorite combination of fresh lobster and tender steak.

Matthew Klein

Keith Glasgow

America prides itself on the assembly line, and fast food is the culinary baby of this industrial land. Although some fast food restaurants offer healthier food such as salads or chicken, the primary items purchased are hamburgers, french fries, and fizzy drinks.

McDonald's

TAKE-OUT AND FAST-FOOD

Take-out has become one of the most successful food-service operations. In the first three months of 1984, seventy million Americans had pizza delivered while seventy-four million others ate Oriental or gourmet take-out fast-foods. Stores selling fresh-baked cookies and premium "European-style" ice creams encourage grazing. Supermarkets prepare ready-made meals, caterers are on every corner, and restaurants offer the choice of their table or yours. Take-out food mirrors the nation's infatuation with *au courant* cuisines. These food fads range from tortellini salad and ratatouille to sushi and guacamole. Gourmet take-out was devised as the working mother's alternative to deli food, but it has since so caught on that people are proud to say they've purchased rather than cooked.

Grilled chicken, stuffed potatoes, pita breads and bagels, falafel, couscous, tabbouleh, calamari, vegetarian lasagna, pasta salad tossed in hot dressings with fresh herbs, steamed vegetables glossed in sesame oil, food-on-the-run items like ham-and-brie sandwiches, dim sum steamed pork buns, egg rolls, cold soups, vegetarian chilies, sesame noodles, and chicken spiced with teriyaki, ginger, or tandoori— served whole or in salads—are on the list of the *très chic* to-go. Salad bars are now in almost every supermarket and produce store in major cities, and they serve hot foods as well as the standard green leaf.

Meanwhile, traditional fast-food has dramatically changed since McDonald's first opened in a Chicago suburb in 1955 with the fifteen-cent hamburger. The notion of providing Americans with efficient and frugal meals is still the idea behind the fried chicken, pizza, and hamburger chains. But they are sprucing up their menus and restaurants to overcome a junk-food image. Many fast-food establishments offer lighter, healthier comestibles like salad bars, multigrain buns, leaner beef, and chicken. One notable twist is serving breakfast—perhaps the last surviving meal in the home-cooked food school. The Egg McMuffin, the Croissanwich, and French toast sticks lure Americans to McDonald's, Burger King, and Arby's in the early morning hours. Fast-food chains specializing in regional and ethnic fare are also found with the likes of New Meiji serving Oriental in California and Popeye's offering Cajun-style fried chicken in the East.

Another American standby, frozen food, used to mean overdone vegetables, tough

Susan M. Duane

Kelin Glasgow

turkey buried in questionable brown sauce, and glutenous potatoes in an aluminum plate. Now it is haute cuisine in a plastic bag—boiled to heat and served on the finest hotel china. This meal-in-a-pouch, which was pioneered by Gerard Rubaud in Vermont, can consist of foie gras, grilled Norwegian salmon with fresh asparagus in red pepper sauce, mousse, and apple tarts. It is described as having the potential to upgrade fast-food to a four-star dining experience. The American consumer seems to like upgrading, as is evidenced by the amount of portion-controlled frozen gourmet foods with French names affixed for gourmand affirmation.

In the end, however, it is the chef-celebrities who set trends—by voicing opinions, creating specialty dishes, and leaving trails of their creative talents across

the nation. They are abetted by a rise in cottage-industry, dairy farms and farmers' markets which are the purveyors of herbs, game, wild mushrooms, and livestock. There are even detectives of sorts who make it their job to unearth new American foods and dishes. Most chefs are also proprietors of their own restaurants. From California to New York and Michigan to Texas, Louisiana and Florida, restaurants with star-status chefs attract people from across the country to sample their fare. The predominant entrée: fish. The theme: classic foods turned upside down by new ingredients and novel preparation. Rabbit sausage with mole sauce, scaloppine of fish with cilantro, oranges, and sun-dried tomatoes, cornmeal pancakes, fried boletus mushrooms in oil and garlic, grilled Santa Barbara quail with Maui onions on a bed of mache with tiny shoestring potatoes, scallops with ginger white wine sauce and deep fried shreds of ginger, egg pasta with duck and fresh figs, red pepper puree seasoned with lemon grass, crawfish "popcorn," and plantains with caviar, sour cream, onions, and refried beans are some of the signature dishes.

Above: *A Chandon is a moderately priced California champagne that rivals some of the best imports.* Right: *New England clam chowder made rich with cream, butter, and the surprising addition of tender bay scallops is an American specialty.*

DRINK

Though white wine is the most popular beverage accompanying restaurant meals, nonalcoholic drinking is the national trend. Americans are drinking more soda than ever. The market is flooded with four brands of Coke, and chocolate soda, a relic of the soda fountain, is back in the form of canned diet chocolate fudge concoctions. Nutrasweet—the brand name for Aspartame, which doesn't have the aftertaste of previous artificial sweeteners—is increasing sales of diet drinks. On the natural side, soft drinks are adding juice. There are juice-flavored and real chocolate sodas such as R.J. Corr's gourmet white chocolate carbonated drink. The 1980s have rediscovered water, and imported sparkling waters compete with America's own. Forty brands of wine coolers—7 percent alcohol, carbonated, fruit-flavored drinks—add to the growing list of alternatives to the more potent form of crushed grape. Nonalcoholic and low-potency beers are now popular, and dealcoholized white wine is also on the market. In addition, California produces a wonderful unfermented sparkling cider. As for coffees and teas, the finest fresh ground beans and imported loose leaves—decaffeinated and brewed with the newest equipment—can be found in the smallest kitchens. While teatime is in, plain tea is boring. Breakfast, darjeeling, rosehips, camomile, and peppermint are popular. Flavored coffees such as almond liqueur and orange are supplanting the after-dinner drink, and people are roasting their own green beans.

For those who still enjoy alcoholic beverages, wine has replaced the cocktail. America's interest in the juice of the grape has resulted in a cultivation of vineyards across the country. It is acceptable to choose an Eastern Long Island or Seattle, Washington wine over the standard French or Italian label. But California still reigns supreme among its American competitors because its available land and climate allow for a constant crop of new vintners. There are the popular jug wines from large companies like Gallo and Inglenook, but the small vineyards such as Dry Creek in Sonoma, Glen Ellen in Mendocino, Zaca Mesa in Santa Barbara, Cloz Duval in Napa, Chateau St. Jean in Alexander Valley, and Mirassou in Monterey County, to name just a few, provide America with an understanding that its own fertile valley soils and warm Western sun can produce a drink to

All over America wineries are springing up, bottling their own red, white, and sparkling wine.

impress the most conservative enologist. The Cabernet Sauvignon is one of California's most successful red grapes, but the Zinfandel is the most widely planted. Chardonnay is the white most consumed, with Chenin Blanc following. But the greatest success story has been the Fumé Blanc or Sauvignon grape. Blush wines—so named because of their color—are made from red grapes such as Zinfandel or Pinot Noir, with the skins, pulp, and seed removed just before the liquid is darkened. This results in a tremendously popular wine that tastes like a white with more flavor than a Chenin Blanc, lacks the flowery bouquet of a rosé, and boasts a lower alcohol content. The Sutter Home Winery is generally credited with pioneering the blush wine with their White Zinfandel. Beaujolais comes in two seasonal waves, but the nouveau, which hits the stores in November and December with premier wines, is the cause for many a dinner party. Champagnes, particularly pink ones, are the incoming sensation. Then there are the vintners who carry on the American spirit of experimentation with the likes of pear and pineapple wines.

Though sales have declined, beer is still a fundamental American drink. From upstate New York's Genessee brewery's Cream Ale to Pennsylvania's Yuengling brewery—the oldest in the United States—to the Great Lakes regions, Americans have put their stamp on a good head of foam. Nationally marketed beers like Wisconsin's Pabst, Schlitz, and Miller, and St. Louis' Michelob and Budweiser are standard American brew. Coors makes unpasteurized beer, which provides greater character. Produced in the world's largest brewery, this Colorado beer is readily available. Some say that malt liquor is an indigenous American beverage, but the Californian "steam beer," now produced in San Francisco, has the most distinctive characteristics. The other beer of interest is from Seattle, and salutes a tall mountain, Rainier. In the 1970s, revivalists started small breweries in much the same way that vineyards were pioneered. Interesting bitter and bottle-conditioned ale came from Sonoma's New Albion and New York City's New Amsterdam.

Like beer, certain hard liquors smack of America and its history. Whiskey is synonymous with Bourbon, though a 1964 act of Congress protected Bourbon's product

Keith Glasgow

Americans are the second biggest importers of tea, left, *and they are credited with inventing both the tea bag (which some tea drinkers look at with disdain) and iced tea. "I'll take a Bud" is a familiar request and Budweiser,* below, *brews one of the most readily available beers. While mixed drinks prevail as popular after work refreshers,* right, *the national trend is to drink white wine to unwind.*

name and insured that its principal home remain the land of green grass and running horses—Kentucky. Rye is another distinctive-quality American whiskey; the difference is that rye is substituted for the maize in Bourbon. "Sour mash" whiskey is the most superior and costly kind, and there are only two distilleries in the United States that produce it. The oldest distillery in the United States, Jack Daniels, has a sour mash recipe that uses fresh spring water from a nearby cave in a limestone cliff. The largest-selling of simple whiskeys, which

require no more than 20 percent of 100 proof, two-year-old whiskey, is Seven Crowns American Whiskey from the Seagram Company—the biggest producer and marketer of spirits in the world. Southern Comfort has a mysterious and haunting peach flavor of the South. It originated in New Orleans but is made in St. Louis. Nassau Royale, a cane-based, citrus-flavored drink with subtle coffee flavors, was invented by an American in Nassau.

The cocktail or mixed drink gained popularity and fame in the United States as a

Sandra Dos Passos

Judd Pilossof

direct result of prohibition—hooch had to be mixed with something to disguise the taste and smell. The first book on cocktails was written by Californian Jerry Thomas and was called *The Bon Vivant's Guide or How to Mix Drinks*. The dry martini, an international symbol of the cocktail hour, was invented at the Knickerbocker Hotel in New York City in 1910. The highball originated in St. Louis in the late nineteenth century as a speedily made drink named for the warning ball placed on a pole for the engineer when his train has to rush to pass an oncoming train. The daiquiri was concocted for American engineers in Cuba, the Gibson was named after the American artist, Charles Dana Gibson, and the Manhattan—devised in Maryland to revive a wounded duelist in 1846—was improved in New York by the addition of sweet vermouth. Mint juleps are as traditional to the South as antebellum mansions and magnolias, and old-fashioneds were created for race fans in Louisville. The pickup drink that has the greatest history is the prairie oyster—two shots of brandy, two teaspoons each of Worcestershire sauce and wine vinegar, one dash cayenne pepper, salt, and one egg yolk blended and drunk with an unbroken yolk on top. An interesting legend tells of the first prairie oyster: One of two United States pioneers of the Old West fell sick and deliriously cried out for oysters. His friend mixed wild turkey eggs with whiskey, and the sick one recovered. It was good reason for a raised glass and traditional toast which is now the proverbial receipt of all American cuisine: "Here's To Your Health!"

Keith Glasgow

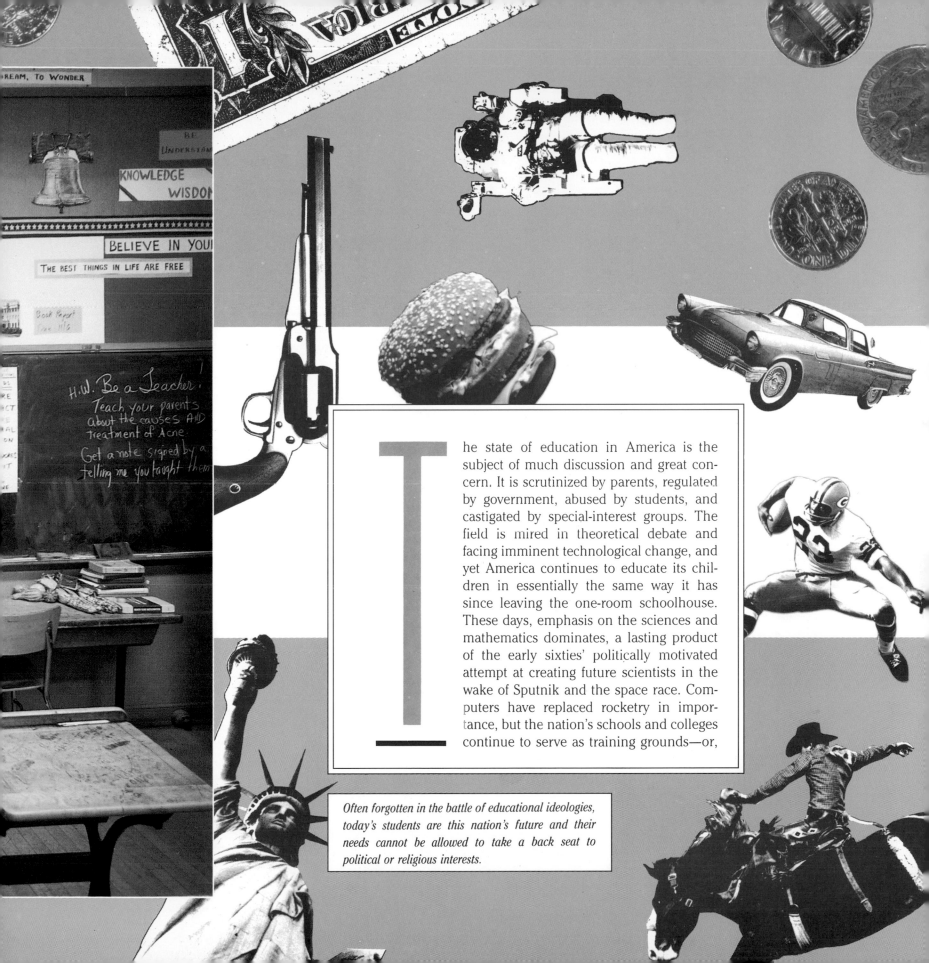

The state of education in America is the subject of much discussion and great concern. It is scrutinized by parents, regulated by government, abused by students, and castigated by special-interest groups. The field is mired in theoretical debate and facing imminent technological change, and yet America continues to educate its children in essentially the same way it has since leaving the one-room schoolhouse. These days, emphasis on the sciences and mathematics dominates, a lasting product of the early sixties' politically motivated attempt at creating future scientists in the wake of Sputnik and the space race. Computers have replaced rocketry in importance, but the nation's schools and colleges continue to serve as training grounds—or,

Often forgotten in the battle of educational ideologies, today's students are this nation's future and their needs cannot be allowed to take a back seat to political or religious interests.

Jerry Howard/Positive Images

Little has changed in the methods of education since the one-room schoolhouse. In an attempt to entertain students, teachers may well be ignoring the fundamentals needed to develop literate, cultured, and inquisitive minds.

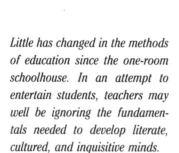

Library of Congress

essentially, vocational schools—for goal-oriented careerists. Such curricula may better prepare students for their future jobs, but it is producing a generation with startlingly little knowledge of, or interest in, world affairs, the arts, or the history of its culture and civilization.

In the early eighties, one of America's most controversial issues was the condition of its educational system. Stories of illiterate high school graduates drew attention to the plight of neglected students, while teachers' unions argued for pay based on merit instead of seniority alone. Educators argued amongst themselves on theoretical matters, practically forgetting about the students in the classrooms. In the void, political and religious interest groups stepped in to exert pressure on teachers and textbook publishers. The ensuing chaos was finally made the focus of a Department of Education report, released in 1983, entitled "A Nation at Risk: The Imperative for Educational Reform."

As a result of "A Nation at Risk" and other alarming reports, some organizations began redressing the problems in educating young Americans. Programs trying to keep troubled teenagers in city schools is just one sign of practical attempts at helping. When celebrities such as Bill Cosby and corporations such as McDonald's join forces to combat educational dilemmas, more attention is paid to these problems. Dry educational theory may speak to grander scales, but corporate backing and identifiable celebrities prove more immediately successful. While school reform remains "theoretical rather than active" (according to the *New York Times*), there is at least hope that the small gains being made now can lead to greater efforts in the future.

Unfortunately, primary (kindergarten through the sixth grade) and secondary (junior and senior high school) education

Jerry Howard/Positive Images

Teacher I know!

Library of Congress

are easily the most influenced by the forces of government and public debate. Over 85 percent of America's children attend public schools, which makes their operation an important concern to most adults. As a result, primary and secondary schools have become ideological battlegrounds for a number of social, political, and religious controversies. Here all segments of society are brought together in an ongoing attempt to find answers that will assuage as many as possible. In the end, the only thing that is agreed upon is that no one seems to be agreeing.

A major debate that has centered on an examination of the quality and purpose of public schools involves the No Pass/No Play controversy. No Pass/No Play laws demand that only students who pass their courses may participate in extracurricular activities. In many communities, athletic accomplishment is a much greater concern than academic success. In Texas, for example, the prospect of a starting quarterback being benched because he earned an "F" in French raises much protest. The result of this battle will be a telling reflection on the future and purpose of secondary institutions in America. At stake is the priority of education in the schools.

Another major battle in the field of education is also one of the oldest. It revolves

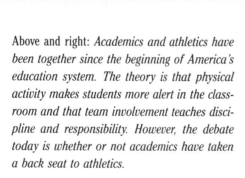

Above and right: *Academics and athletics have been together since the beginning of America's education system. The theory is that physical activity makes students more alert in the classroom and that team involvement teaches discipline and responsibility. However, the debate today is whether or not academics have taken a back seat to athletics.*

Robert Landau

Reid Calanan

Gayle Jann

Reid Calanan

Hans Neleman/Wheeler Pictures

While the value of a college diploma in America may have changed, other pursuits remain as popular as ever.

around the teaching of human origins to students and essentially has pitted the scientific community against political conservatives and a number of religious figures. Since the Scopes "Monkey Trial," creationists and evolutionists have battled over biology and anthropology/archaeology. The early eighties saw pressure from conservative watch-groups on book publishers to temper science texts' handling of evolution and give equal time to biblical versions of creation.

Recently, however, the scientific community, backed by educators and political liberals, has scored important victories in its attempts to improve the "accuracy" of textbooks. Decisions in Texas and California have paved the way for a more scientific handling of the subject, which has implications for all American students. Since publishers create texts to be sold throughout the country, they try to make them as "safe" as possible. As the most conservative states ease their restrictions, publishers will be able to produce textbooks that are deemed more accurate by scientists in the respective fields involved.

Religious conservatives, in particular, also found themselves fighting for tuition credits for private schools. Led by the Secretary of Education, William Bennett, several groups—including parochial and secular private schools—essentially have fought to give government money that would have been spent on children in public schools to their parents to subsidize private-school tuitions. Many argue that this will create dwindling funds for public schools, forcing more students to private schools. The spiral relationship could well create a country where only the poor still attend public schools, and where there's not enough money left to educate them since so much will be going to private schools.

While parochial schools, representing the majority of private institutions, would

Keith Glasgow

be the most obvious beneficiaries of the tuition tax credits, the increasing number of middle- and upper-middle-class families sending their children to private schools (particularly at the secondary level) would also benefit. With a stronger secondary educational background many of these families and their children will opt for affordable public universities instead of the considerably more expensive, prestigious private colleges. The rise of several fine state university systems has been one of the greatest changes in the condition of higher education. They are making it possible for more people to attend college than ever before.

Indeed, an unprecedented three out of five high school graduates are going on to a higher level of study, and the number of older individuals returning to education is also on the rise. Housewives, laborers, and others are going back to the classroom for degrees that one Department of Education report called "the basic credential for an ever-growing number of occupations as well as a necessary criterion for leadership in virtually all walks of life." Unfortunately, this emphasis on preprofessional training has turned many schools into glorified vocational training centers and redirected the original emphasis of higher education.

The concentration on career-oriented courses has recently raised questions about the future of liberal arts instruction. The Secretary of Education himself has criticized American colleges and universities for failing to provide students with a "core of common studies." Bennett is one of many who believe that the history of our civilization, based on a "careful reading of several masterworks of English, American, and European literature," is an essential part of higher education. Some argue that Bennett's opinions are based on a desire to reestablish an elitism that separated college graduates of the past from their "less cul-

An emphasis on career-oriented curriculum has made it increasingly necessary for students to investigate alternative areas of learning during college.

Keith Glasgow

The idyllic campus life of Harvard remains the goal for many students hoping to turn an Ivy League degree into a successful career.

tured" contemporaries. But, as a college education has become available to more and more people, the practicality of esoteric learning has lessened. More and more institutions are relying on a preprofessional emphasis to attract students.

In America, the eighteen-to-twenty-four-year-old population (the focus of college-enrollment predictions) is steadily decreasing. While the Ivy League and other prestigious universities continue to choose from the best applicants, less well-known private schools are beginning to have trouble getting, and holding onto, students. Advertisements on rock radio stations and other youth-oriented media are one sign of the push to attract potential students.

At a time when tuitions eclipse the ten thousand-dollar level and the cost of room, board, and tuition totals fifteen thousand dollars, most families are finding it necessary to seek out various aid and loan programs. Realizing this, even the most selective and respected colleges have expanded their work-study programs, low-interest loans, and even scholarships. Guaranteed Student Loans are almost automatically available to families earning less than thirty thousand dollars a year, offering interest charges far lower than current rates. The GSL and other government-subsidized loans have made pursuing a degree easier for millions. In addition, the attitude of Americans toward being in debt has changed

Wellesley College

Stuart Cohen

drastically from that of previous generations, who felt uncomfortable owing anything to anyone.

Unfortunately, there have been a number of problems in collecting on many of these loans. In the seventies, defaulting on such loans was a common practice, and few were caught or punished. But the government has since clamped down on these individuals and made it tougher to get away with defaulting. Recent laws allowing income-tax returns to be withheld from such individuals is just one step that has been taken in collecting millions of unpaid loans, which can then be relent to current college students. From the local community colleges to universities with popula-tions of forty thousand or more, a whole new financial structure is being born. America's graduates are more plentiful than ever before, but they are saddled with debts that they will paying off until it's time to send their own children to college.

In summary, America is currently educating more people, to higher levels, than ever before. Unfortunately, like any industry that expands to produce in greater quantity, the quality has suffered. A concern with ideologies, politics, and religion has become so complex and pervasive that America's future—its students—is being neglected. Many suggestions have been made to correct this situation, but it remains to be seen what will actually be done.

From the lab to the stadium: Colleges and universities continue to serve as microcosms of the outside world. Some maintain that they have become glorified vocational training centers, while others see much to cheer about.

THE GREAT OUTDOORS

Don Renner/Photo Trends

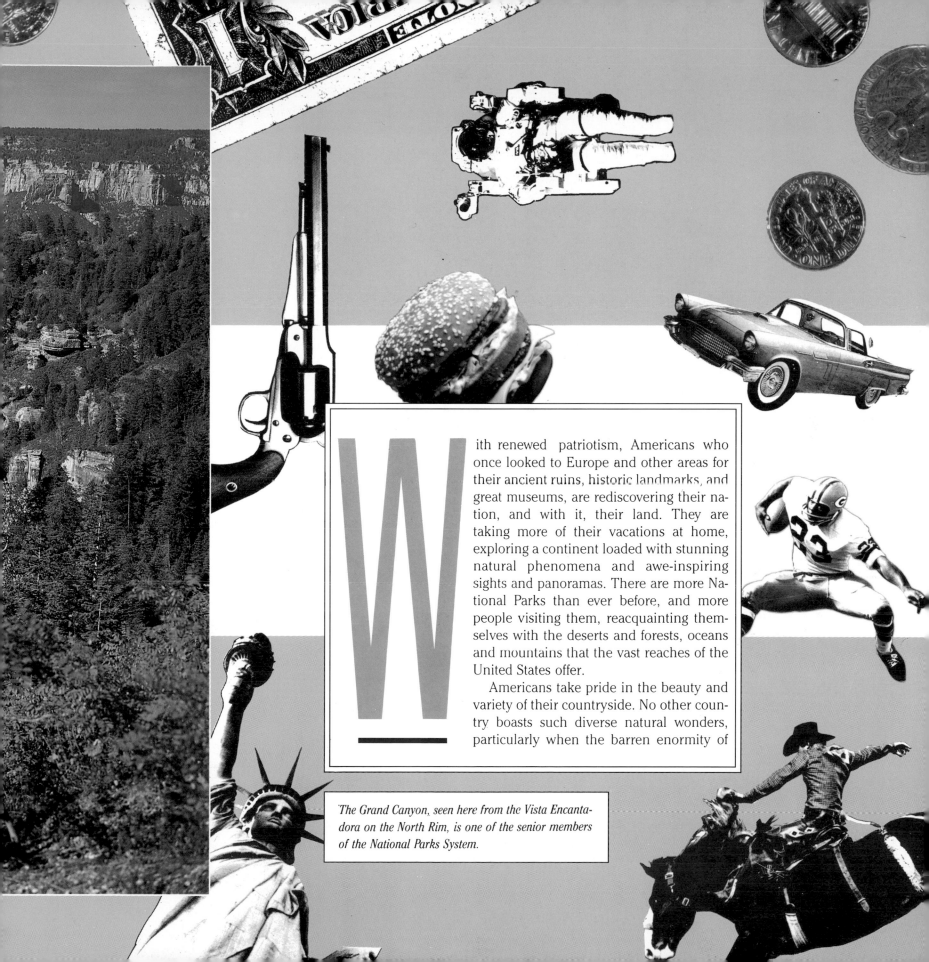

With renewed patriotism, Americans who once looked to Europe and other areas for their ancient ruins, historic landmarks, and great museums, are rediscovering their nation, and with it, their land. They are taking more of their vacations at home, exploring a continent loaded with stunning natural phenomena and awe-inspiring sights and panoramas. There are more National Parks than ever before, and more people visiting them, reacquainting themselves with the deserts and forests, oceans and mountains that the vast reaches of the United States offer.

Americans take pride in the beauty and variety of their countryside. No other country boasts such diverse natural wonders, particularly when the barren enormity of

The Grand Canyon, seen here from the Vista Encantadora on the North Rim, is one of the senior members of the National Parks System.

The incredible diversity of America's natural treasures offers a wide range of options, from the desolate beauty of Arizona's Monument Valley, left, *to the lush growth of Hawaii's tropical islands,* below, *or the damp wonder of Washington's rain forests, such as this one,* far right, *within Olympic National Park.*

Robert Landau

John Dominis/Wheeler Pictures

Alaska and tropical beauty of Hawaii are included. On the mainland, the Rocky Mountain chain starts within the Arctic Circle in Alaska and cuts through numerous parks in the Lower Forty-eight. The Appalachians run through Shenandoah National Park and others along the Eastern Seaboard. Between them, and sloping down off of them on the other sides, are deserts, gorges, salt flats, alluvial plains, bayous, beaches, islands, and lakes—a bonanza of scenic wonders words cannot adequately describe.

Conservationists began extolling America's natural treasures in the early nineteenth century, and the Yellowstone Act of 1872 set aside more than two million acres "as a public park or pleasuring-ground for the benefit and enjoyment of the people." It was the first example of large-scale natural preservation in the world, at a time when land was still seen as a limitless commodity. Since then, another seventy-seven million acres have been added to the protected lands. The National Parks System has expanded to include a total of forty-nine parks and nearly three hundred system areas that include monuments, preserves, scenic trails, riverways, battlefields, and even a solitary tree in Kansas.

Despite the encroachment of civilization into all parts of the United States, which has threatened the boundaries of the parks, the National Parks System has continued to improve and expand. The sixties and the seventies were good times for conservationists, as one-third of the current park system was acquired then. Some of the most pristine, undisturbed wilderness in North America was added during these boom years, areas still being discovered by serious explorers and adventurous tourists.

However, in the well-known parks, overcrowding is a growing concern. Grand Canyon, Rocky Mountain, Acadia, and other senior members of the parks system are battling the strain of more visitors. To alleviate this problem, the lesser-known parks are being more widely publicized and attempts are being made to make them less primitive and more accessible. Whether this might lead to similar overcrowding problems in the newer parks remains to be seen, but the short-term benefits justify the risk.

One of the parks that remains unknown to most Americans, but is receiving more publicity, is Minnesota's Voyageurs National Park. Established in 1975, it contains more than two hundred thousand untouched acres, but receives relatively few visitors. Voyageurs borders Canada, with its headquarters in International Falls (a town so cold in winter it was once featured in a commercial for car batteries that could start under any conditions). In warm weather, Voyageurs' lakes and small islands contain "a fantastic wildlife show ranging from bald eagles to moose and bears."

The North Cascades National Park was established in 1968 in Washington State, also just south of the Canadian border. Its jagged portion of the Rocky Mountain chain is the home of glaciers, ice falls, lush forests, and, again, spectacular wildlife. North Cascades' precipitous surroundings make it difficult to reach, but this difficult terrain fortunately keeps development away. Therefore, services in North Cascades are few, but anyone looking for unspoiled solitude will find it in abundance.

Yet nothing in the continental United States can approach the immensity and purity of the lands recently designated part of the National Parks System in Alaska. "The Great Land" is the last American wilderness frontier, and the sheer enormity of its natural wonders dwarfs anything in the Lower Forty-eight.

Alaska boasts Mt. McKinley, the highest peak in North America, as well as the Malaspina Glacier, a mass of ice larger than

the state of Rhode Island. The Malaspina is a small part of the Wrangell-St. Elias National Park and Reserve, the largest unit in the National Parks System. Yellowstone, Grand Canyon, Yosemite, Everglades, Glacier, and Death Valley National Parks could fit within the borders of Wrangell-St. Elias, with room to spare. Abutting Canada between Juneau and Anchorage, the park links the southern arm of Alaska with the massive peninsula that reaches into the Arctic Circle to the north and across the International Date Line to the west.

Mt. McKinley, in turn, is part of Denali National Park and Preserve. This park, 4.7 million acres huge (4.2 million acres *less* than Wrangell-St. Elias), was first established around the twenty-thousand-foot peak, and grew exponentially with the passage in 1980 of the Alaska National Interest Lands Conservation Act (ANILCA), the most important piece of legislation in the history of the National Parks System. ANILCA resulted from one of the key environmental battles that took place in the seventies. A battle to protect Alaskan country against the pipeline and the state's extensive oil operations, which are a fact of life today, the legislation set aside tens of millions of unspoiled acres. Lake Clark National Park is another tremendous parcel of land protected by the ANILCA. It is the size of Connecticut, is reached most easily by plane, and contains active volcanoes and a lake forty miles in length. Visitors ride the Charley River through the Yukon-Charley Rivers National Preserve; it's so remote that boats are brought in by helicopter to be dropped off anywhere along its 115-mile length.

Farther north, Gates of the Arctic and its neighboring parks, all entirely north of the Arctic Circle, contain some of the most desolate, and to some, most challenging land on the globe. The parks include arctic valleys, wild rivers, and uncounted lakes. However, there are no camping facilities

Jeff Schultz

Jeff Schultz

Cross-country skiing and other winter sports are bringing record numbers of Americans to nature during what had once been a slow season for the national parks.

Bald eagles take refuge in an Alaskan cottonwood tree. "The Great Land" is home to a number of endangered species rarely seen in the Lower Forty-eight.

Jeff Schultz

The Lands Conservation Act of 1980 more than doubled the amount of parklands in America. Now there is enough room for both wildlife and humans to pursue their respective needs.

Michael Melford/Wheeler Pictures

anywhere in Gates of the Arctic, and no nearby hotels, though there are guided tours featuring treks through the last true American frontier.

It may be that the lack of facilities and their remoteness will allow many Alaskan parks to remain relatively undisturbed and natural. With time, however, encroachment is inevitable. Besides attracting more and more visitors every year, the minerals beneath Alaska's scenic, if desolate, vistas are also increasingly desirable. It is hopeful, however, that Americans have learned a lesson and will fight to protect the land as they necessarily accommodate the demands of men.

Parallel to their growing fascination with Alaska, Americans are also discovering winter sports. From ice fishing to cross-country skiing to snowmobiling, they are finding scores of ways to enjoy nature in the cold. The popularity of cross-country skiing has introduced many to the pleasures of a journey through beautiful, snow-covered acreage otherwise inaccesible during the winter months. With visitors also participating in downhill skiing, hiking/snow-shoeing, and snowmobiling, there is a year-round flow of visitors to many parks. Yosemite's Badger Pass and Rocky Mountains' Ski Estes are downhill facilities that draw skiers from across the country. Snow-

mobiling through the Grand Tetons' "Potholes" plain or Acadia's back roads is enticing more participants than ever. Twenty years ago, barely five thousand visitors came to Yellowstone in the winter; the total could soon exceed fifty thousand for a single season of fun on snow and ice.

It should be noted, however, that the increase in off-season use of the parks concerns many environmentalists. Resources already strained by the constant flow of summer visitors have less time to recover, while hibernating animals are also subject to disturbance. There is no argument that the parks are enjoyable at all times of the year, but as one conservation-

With the growing popularity of off-season pursuits such as cross-country skiing, above, *the Grand Tetons,* left, *have become a year-round attraction.*

Geoffrey C. Clifford/Wheeler Pictures

Rivers, lakes, oceans: America's bodies of water are as diverse as the land. The melting snows of the Rocky Mountains, *right*, provide a startling contrast to a quite lake, *below,* or the fury of the Atlantic Ocean pounding against the rocky shore of Maine's Acadia National Park.

Randy O'Rourke

Benjamin Dimmit

Gayle Jann

Manuel Dos Passos

Benjamin Dimmit

Every year scores of travelers visit Vermont, above, *to witness the changing seasons in one of America's most magnificent autumn landscapes. Fiery reds and vibrant yellows electrify the rolling hills. Dramatically silhouetted by the sun, these massive, skin-smooth sand dunes,* center, *are alive with light and shadow. In order to preserve this awe-inspiring scene, many states have made it illegal to disturb the dunes.*

ist put it, "One must question whether the parks can or should try to be all things to all people. For example, is it necessary—or even appropriate—for our great natural parks to provide such a diversity of recreational activities?"

Americans have a continuing legacy of enjoyment of nature in all its glory, as far removed from the tainting influence of civilization as possible. Thoreau's musings from Walden Pond and the early photographers who ventured into unknown wilderness were the first to capture America's fascination with the land. People marveled at the breathtaking views and unimaginable grandeur of the first photos brought back to the cities. Around the turn of this century, photographers such as Timothy O'Sullivan and Eadweard Muybridge (also

known for his early, pre-moving-pictures study of men in motion) introduced Americans to natural wonders they had only heard about until then.

The late Ansel Adams, the world's best-known nature photographer, is revered for his black-and-white photographs that evoke memories of these earliest nature photographs. Though Adams' own skills are undeniable, his decision to work predominantly in black-and-white landscapes may have had much to do with the chord his work has struck in Americans. In Adams' photographs there is an impression of timelessness and isolation that captures the contemplative ideal that many Americans instill in nature. The great outdoors is outside of time, a place where people can go to escape the modern world.

Tumbling over moss-covered rocks into a pool of water, this beautiful waterfall at Baxter State Park is a peaceful destination for weary hikers.

Gayle Jann

CHAPTER 8

FILM, TELEVISION, and RADIO

FILM

The buzzword of the American film industry is "high tech"; the catchphrase is "movie brats"—a generation of film school trained directors such as Steven Spielberg, George Lucas, and Brian DePalma with borderline influence of Martin Scorsese and Francis Ford Coppola. The combination of this industry lingo and shrewd marketing has created the blockbuster film.

During the 1970s, American filmmakers were reacting to Vietnam, Woodstock, Watergate, and the upheaval America experienced in the 1960s. The new directors of the 1970s focused on realism combined with a political energy and irreverence

Star Wars captured the imaginations of a whole generation of Americans with its space-age setting and fantastical adventure. A huge box office success, the "Force" (and George Lucas) continued into several sequels that also met with tremendous favor.

Robert Landau

Above: *In the 1970s, disaster films were popular. But* Jaws, *the story of a man-eating white shark, was a combination disaster-horror film with adventure and family-oriented drama.* Right: *At Universal Studios, this house was designed to burn permanently, even after the box-office sales had waned.*

reminiscent of the past decade. Films reflected big business, government, American gluttony for power, the hero as villain and outcast, confused religious zeal and altruism, and an America torn between its past and seemingly enticing future. The work of these new directors promoted the idea of director as "auteur"; more than author or actor, these directors were the creative genius behind the films. Coppola *(The Godfather, Apocalypse Now)* introduced larger-than-life storytelling as a popular format—a springboard for the fantasy films of Spielberg *(E.T., Close Encounters of the Third Kind)* and Lucas *(Star Wars)*. John Cassavetes' *(Minnie & Moskowitz, A Woman Under the Influence)* and Martin Scorsese's use of the camera *(Taxi Driver, Alice Doesn't Live Here Anymore)*, and Robert Altman's dialogue *(M.A.S.H., Nashville)* evoked a new style of jolting realism. Woody Allen *(Annie Hall, Manhattan)* adjusted romance to incorporate a modern twist: the mildly neurotic love affair with a bittersweet ending. Other prominent directors who contributed to the idea of director as creative sorcerer or "auteur" were Paul Mazursky *(Bob & Carol & Ted & Alice, An Unmarried Woman)*, Michael Ritchie *(The Candidate, Smile)*, and Hal Ashby *(Harold and Maude, Coming Home)*. The personal filmmaking era evolved and touched on divorce in *Kramer vs. Kramer* and family struggles in *Ordinary People* and *Terms of Endearment*. The "women's genre" was updated to cover the dilemma of making a choice between career and children in *The Turning Point* and the bonding of female friendship in *Julia*. In the 1980s, even men emerged as feminists as Dustin Hoffman grappled with life-in-drag in *Tootsie*—the male with the feminine point of view. Simple-folk-farm-flicks became vogue with *Tender Mercies, Country, Places in the Heart,* and *The River*.

With a knowledge of Hollywood's history, the emerging directors also made nostalgia a genre. George Lucas resurrected the 1950s in *American Graffiti,* and Spielberg recaptured the 1950s fascination with UFOs and a sense of childlike wonderment in *Close Encounters of the Third Kind.* Stereotypes reversed, high school hoods became heros, and flying saucers were the bearers of friendly aliens. Mel Brooks made the Hollywood western and the horror film comedy subjects in *Blazing Saddles* and *Young Frankenstein.* Sequels and remakes were extremely popular, and cartoon heroes were reincarnated. Woody Allen's *The Purple Rose of Cairo* captured Hollywood during the Depression era in the form of a celluloid character come to life. *The Big Chill* topped off what *American Graffiti* started—it presented a reflection of the reflecting glass—America saw itself being nostalgic.

By 1977 box-office demographics were changing—tickets were now being sold to those under the age of twenty-five. The evolving youth films were escapist, patriotic, and verging on post-Vietnam militarism. *Rocky*'s acclaim can be attributed to the storm of red-white-and-blue that surrounded the 1976 Olympics and Bicentennial. The film's surefire premise for success was to make America feel positive. *Star Wars* followed as the epitome of the Hollywood product—a composite of romance, disaster, high technology, comedy, drama, and militarism. The new trick: a 1930s Capra-like *(It's a Wonderful Life, You Can't Take It With You)* enthusiasm for life, with a religious moral tagged to the fable. "The Force Be With You!" became a widely used modern salutation.

One of the great escapist innovations of the 1970s was the disaster film as typified by Spielberg's modification of the genre, *Jaws.* Its appeal to America's youth was found in the film's hero, a figure who would have been unheard of as a protagonist ten

Right: *John Belushi's antics in* The Blues Brothers *and* Animal House *films made him a favorite of the youth market, while Woody Allen,* below, *began as a comedian with a wider range and developed into a humorist known for his examinations of pathos and romance.*

Below: *Oscar, the statue given at the annual Academy Awards Ceremony, is a much coveted prize because it greatly boosts box office sales.* Right: *Madonna, queen of pop records and video, made her film debut in the independent production of* Desperately Seeking Susan.

Robert Landau

Warner Bros., Inc.

years earlier: a family man and cop. But the most creative feature of *Jaws* was the marketing technique. It opened in five hundred theaters simultaneously accompanied by a television-saturation ad campaign, which became a stylized pattern for theatrical film release. The horror genre also underwent a surge of popularity that was legitimized by Brian DePalma's *Carrie*. Soundtrack tie-ins became a norm for the promotion of the musical film with *Saturday Night Fever*. This film was the precursor for the 1980s union of film and music in *Fame, Flashdance,* and *Purple Rain*. *Saturday Night Fever*'s alienation theme—age-old to film—has since been updated to portray those more physically than psychologically disengaged. *Beverly Hills Cop, Star Man, Brother from Another Planet, Lost in America,* and *The Purple Rose of Cairo* are films in which the protagonist is stranded in an unfamiliar environment.

As Hollywood targeted movies to specific audiences to insure financial success, an independent film movement took hold. The cult following of the *Rocky Horror Picture Show* unearthed a nontraditional audience. Independents predominantly celebrated regional and ethnic topics ignored by Hollywood, and many films focused on labor or left-wing issues dealing with historical American events. It was Barbara Kopple's *Harlan County U.S.A.*, a direct-cinema-style account of the struggles of coal miners, that ignited interest in alternative films. Since then independents have become increasingly successful, and their topics range from horror flicks and new road films to rock documentaries, many of which make use of a less-than-Hollywood-slick Super-8 New York Film School mode. *Blood Simple, Liquid Sky, Stranger than Paradise,* and *Stop Making Sense* were popularly distributed independent movies. Su-

Richard Litt

san Seidelman's *Desperately Seeking Susan* was the Hollywood success story of an independent filmmaker, as was Hector Babenko's *Kiss of the Spider Woman.* John Sayles' *Return of the Secaucus Seven* became the basis for Hollywood's own version of reunion-nostalgia in *The Big Chill,* which was adapted for an unsuccessful television series called *Hometown.*

The style of American film continues to alter in response to a Hollywood threatened by VCRs and an attrition of the theater audience. But with the surging independents, pay-cable markets, and films made outside of the Los Angeles area, Hollywood's objective is to earn as much as possible from a single release. *Star Wars* is one of the highest-grossing films ever made, while *Beverly Hills Cop* is a studio gem because it captured one out of every three tickets sold in 1984. *Ghostbusters* earned $127 million, making it 1984's big-

gest financial success. However, unlike *Star Wars*—to which the average twelve-year-old returned a dozen times—today's audience will see *Ghostbusters* once, and then wait for its video release. In addition to competition from videos, other monetary losses have hurt the industry. Michael Cimino's *Heaven's Gate,* for example, was the biggest pecuniary disaster in the history of film. Its loss of forty-four million dollars sank the United Artists studio.

The critical speculation is that theatrical film will become more of an event for the VCR, while the blockbuster special-effects movie will still be more appreciated on the big screen. Optimistic movie fans, however, deny that theatrical film is passé. Theater's advantage over the VCR is its ability to provide a sense of community; there's nothing like sharing a laugh with an audience at a Woody Allen comedy, or the teary-eyed respect for a film like *The Killing Fields.*

Grade B horror flicks have serious cult followings, and the Rocky Horror Picture Show has become a traditional midnight affair for fans who come dressed as the characters. It's quite a departure from the clean-cut Elvis Presley movies of the 1950s.

TELEVISION

Television's advantage over film is its production schedule, which allows for the immediate broadcast of popular ideals that reflect the national mood. A disadvantage for television is that it is always a step behind in creating what is up-and-coming because it panders to the majority and can never quite pinpoint its audience. In its short history, television has evolved from live dramatic programs to ones that utilize laugh tracks and pat-formula situation comedies. But the advent of video and home-movie cassettes has undermined TV's notion of prefabricated entertainment, and the live audiences have returned as the sit-coms become less urbane and original movies are produced by the networks.

What's new: dramas dealing with current, controversial issues in the television movie. Miniseries and made-for-TV movies such as "Holocaust," "Something About Amelia," and "The Day After" have gently exposed middle-America to uncomfortable subjects such as nuclear war, incest, wife-beating, alcoholism, and homosexuality. Docudramas fictionalize the news—the creators of "The Atlanta Child Murders" passed judgment on current events. A video-influenced melding of music with drama and high-tech film cutting is increasingly prevalent on dramatic shows like "Miami Vice" and "St. Elsewhere." Other notable developments are the use of strong character relationships in sit-coms, more female and black characters, and nighttime soaps. The supernatural is back in vogue, and the storytelling anthology series is revived from television's golden days. Syndication of game shows has allowed over forty million viewers to make the "Wheel of Fortune" the most-watched program.

The "Saturday Night Live" comedy style

RCA TV

Right: *Television's humble beginnings in the 1950s were rooted in family entertainment, an offshoot of evening radio entertainment.* Below: *Action news is covered with an immediacy that makes the unusual, the spectacular, or the upsetting events of the world a living room reality.*

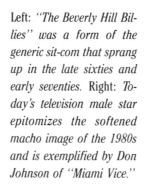

Left: *"The Beverly Hill Billies"* was a form of the generic sit-com that sprang up in the late sixties and early seventies. Right: *Today's television male star epitomizes the softened macho image of the 1980s and is exemplified by Don Johnson of "Miami Vice."*

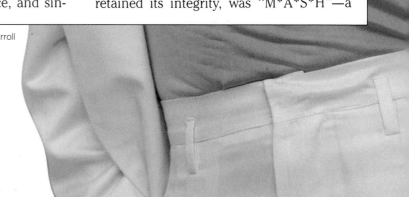

developed on late-night TV appealed to the Young Urban Professional's interest in trivia in a format that poked fun at current events and pop culture. Traditionally, however, the situation comedy has been the small screen's forum for letting America know what's on its mind without getting heavy-handed. It appeals to the family-oriented viewer. The new brand of sit-com has real characters in recognizable situations. "Cheers," "Family Ties," "Kate & Allie," and "The Cosby Show" have bridged the audience gap between prime-time and late-night audiences.

In the 1950s, comedy thrived with Lucille Ball, Jackie Gleason, and Phil Silvers playing to live audiences with stories about the housewife and blue-collar worker. The 1960s gave way to suburban living with Dick Van Dyke. When television introduced the laugh track on shows like "Green Acres" and "The Beverly Hillbillies"—the networks' targeting of some amorphous rural audience—characters became absurd. Norman Lear brought reality back into focus with his own refreshing brand of social satire. "All in the Family," "Maude," "The Jeffersons," and "One Day at a Time" dealt with sexual dilemmas, racial tensions, abortion, divorce, and single parenting. The formula: Replace the notion of a wholesome America with a common social issue, then reduce it to twenty-two minutes of chuckles and occasional poignant lines preceding commercial breaks. America was laughing at itself, but the characters were still caricatures. The Garry Marshall shows that followed—"Happy Days," "Laverne & Shirley," "Mork & Mindy"—avoided social themes and utilized the positive-outlook and alien-fascination motifs popular in feature films like *American Graffiti* and *Star Wars*. A program that was also born of film, but retained its integrity, was "M*A*S*H"—a phenomenon unto itself that lasted seven years and maintains its faithful audience with reruns several times a day. Continuing the irreverence and antimilitarism of the 1960s, "M*A*S*H" also developed a cast of characters whose relationships were the principal hook of the episodes. Similarly, "The Mary Tyler Moore Show," which exhibited the dilemmas of a single woman in the working world, had strong character relationships. It too developed a devoted seven-year following. At the same time, Aaron Spelling introduced "Charlie's Angels," "Three's Company," "Love Boat," and "Fantasy Island"—a series of bland programs that prostituted social themes like women-in-male-work-roles by spicing plots with sex-kitten characters and wish-fulfillment ploys. Nonetheless, they were the popular brand of situation comedy until the 1980s. "The Mary Tyler Moore Show" gave way to "Lou Grant," and MTM went on to produce "Hill Street Blues" and "St. Elsewhere"—all of which tackle social issues in a dramatic context with a provisional amount of comic relief. But it was "The Cosby Show" that revived what seems to be television's vestigial organ, and the sit-com is once again TV's mainstay.

Soap opera dates back to radio with daytime shows like "Search for Tomorrow" and the highly rated "General Hospital" in which Elizabeth Taylor made guest appearances. Nighttime soaps have their foundation in "Peyton Place." But many Americans' obsession with ostentatious lifestyles is giving sociologists substantial cause to surmise that they are well-steeped in a fascination for capitalistic entrepreneurism —or that media marketing tactics have become increasingly sophisticated.

Nighttime soaps are pervading all aspects of American life, and the interest in the real-person milieu has been offset by a voyeuristic passion for the trials and tribulations of the ultrarich and powerful. "Dallas" was the 1978 debut of evening soaps and became the highest-rated show on television. "Who Shot J.R.?" was a question of national importance when the show ended its second season with the mystery of who had fired at the principal character of the wealthy Texas oil family. "Dynasty," the saga of a Denver family's powers, passions, finances, automobiles, and attire, eclipsed the 1984 Presidential inauguration with higher ratings. There are "Dynasty" collections of clothing, sheets, and perfumes sold in department stores. Although these soaps have seen their peak seasons, they have become milestones in television history and are exported around the world.

Along with the nighttime soap phenomenon are the high-tech magazine-style programs such as "PM Magazine," "Entertainment Tonight," and "Lifestyles of the Rich and Famous," which delve into behind-the-scenes gossip about America's celebrated and wealthy. The idea of news as entertainment started with Edward R. Murrow's "Person to Person" and continued into the nightly news, where vivid images of Vietnam, world famine, and other disasters were brought into living rooms with an emphasis on newsfilm. The reporting style developed in the 1970s was candid, with anchorpersons in casual attire exchanging "in" jokes. "Meet the Press"—the oldest series in network television—is a hybrid talk-news show where newsmakers are interviewed by newspaper journalists. CBS introduced "60 minutes" in the Sunday, 7:00 P.M. slot in 1972, changing the face of television news by creating the newsmagazine format. Since its inception, "20/20" and others have tried to duplicate CBS' success. The result is a number of programs made up of short segments on current topics ranging from AIDS to Young Republicans. The emphasis is on the personality of the reporter, with punchy writing, dramatic camera angles, and use of editing that is popular in video. The product is often no better than *People* magazine à la television.

Talk shows have been a favorite format since radio, and the "Today" show is the prototype, with interviews, commentary, and feature stories. "Good Morning America" is its two-hour counterpart with former actor David Hartman as host. Other well-received talk-show personalities are Phil Donahue, who appeals to middle-America and plays devil's advocate with both audience and guests, and Merv Griffin. Dick Cavett appealed to the more sophisticated habitués of public television. Perhaps the most popular late-night talk show is the "Tonight Show," which is hosted by Johnny Carson. He represents the clean-cut Midwesterner with a touch of Peck's Bad Boy, and is one of the highest-paid television personalities today.

For those who feel that American television is a catchall for the banalities of our culture, the Public Broadcasting Service has provided some relief with telecasts of classical, jazz, and operatic music, dance, children's shows, educational programming, and programs imported from England. America's answer to the BBC— where they aren't afraid to produce serious drama—is "American Playhouse," a showcase for quality dramatic productions and an outlet for independent filmmakers. "American Playhouse" presents the works of American writers both past and present, such as Philip Roth, Mark Twain, Sam Shepard, Ntozake Shange, F. Scott Fitzgerald, Tennessee Williams, James Baldwin, John Cheever, and Kurt Vonnegut. In addition, "American Playhouse" is a venue for many new writers. The programming ranges from stories of the Salem witch hunts to tales of nuclear holocaust, depicting America from the Texas farm to the urban street. "Testament," "El Norte," and "Oppenheimer" are some of their notable productions, and all of them challenge the viewer to think about current issues.

The number of stations blossomed in the early 1980s, and today the listed independents are triple what they were when network television began, with affiliate stations steadily increasing. But while the prime-time 7:00 P.M. to 11:00 P.M. slot has a healthy average of eighty-five million viewers, television is feeling the threat of cable and home video. As a result, the networks are seeking out new programming strategies to retain their audience. The modern viewer has a wealth of cable programming and video selection and does not habitually tune in to the same show. To combat this lack of viewer loyalty, the anthology series—a nonepisodic story format popular in the 1950s—is being revived by the networks. It appeals to viewers who don't tune in regularly to any particular program and therefore don't know the steady cast of characters or long-term story line found in most television series. Soaps are likely to revert to the working-class hero as the audience becomes inured to the repetitive sagas of the wealthy. The future promises more fusion of music and drama, and a plethora of female and minority characters. Role reversals, such as that seen in *Tootsie*, will become evident. As the number of viewers continues to decline, networks will vie for the largest share of the audience by narrowing their demographics and increasing original production.

CABLE, MTV, AND VIDEO

Cable's beginnings were humble, and it still has not taken on the popular status of the VCR. Cable originally serviced areas unable to receive television

American Playhouse has been an innovative source of original dramatic productions for television. Here, Jessica Lange plays in Tennessee Williams's "Cat on a Hot Tin Roof." Below: David Letterman's late-night talk show has succeeded in grabbing the audience who wants an outrageous and spontaneous host.

Shecter Cone Communications

transmission, and after several false starts in a twenty-five-year development, pay-cable surfaced as a television alternative—it offered uncut, uninterrupted movies. In 1975, when Home Box Office (HBO) began distributing programming by satellite, cable boomed, and other cable networks covering sports, live entertainment, and the pop music scene began to appear. Americans were subscribing, cities were wired, and homeowners even forked out up to five thousand dollars for a dish antenna. By 1980, cable was in demand in every large American city.

Satellite allowed for low-cost, national distribution and the emergence of cable networks like HBO, SHOWTIME, ESPN, ARTS, BRAVO, DISNEY, and NICKELODEON. Each of these networks specializes programming in areas such as movies, sports, cultural entertainment, and children's shows. SIN is notable as the oldest Spanish language network. In addition to the networks there are superstations WTBS Atlanta, WGW Chicago, and WOR New York, all of which come as part of a pay-cable service and carry old films and sporting events. HBO and SHOWTIME are the most popular networks, though they are losing subscribers as a result of the videocassette boom. CNN Cable News Network has established cable news as a major journalistic contender to network news. Its twenty-four-hour news operation can preempt regular programming to deliver fast-breaking news with a rotating anchor team. Unlike the networks, who pander to the rating results by emphasizing the anchorperson's personality or appearance, CNN's emphasis is on immediate coverage of a story.

MTV became a cultural phenomenon in the early 1980s and is the foremost promoter of rock video. MTV's style: multiple images, angular editing, and surrealistic visual effects, which shrink and expand the picture. MTV's format: a mixture of studio interviews, live concert presentations, music and concert news, and the latest videos.

MTV can be seen in over twenty-four million homes twenty-four hours a day. For those who prefer a softer edge, the creators of MTV have introduced VH-1, which broadcasts more sedate music videos meant to appeal to an older crowd.

The development of rock video rejuvenated a struggling rock industry, and the video has also become a strong influence on other aspects of American life. Politicians study MTV to determine what voters will want, television shows like "Miami Vice," "Hunter," and "St. Elsewhere" have used rock video in their stories, and fashion designers such as Norma Kamali and Stephen Sprouse promote their clothing in videos scored with thumping beats. Films such as *Flashdance* use video segments lifted from the film for promotional purposes, and video-slick commercials sell everything from soap to cars and chocolates. It is not unusual to see film personalities like Jeremy Irons, Ron Howard, Brian DePalma, and John Sayles credited with directing music videos. Rock videos have provided a way to visualize music and give faces to familiar radio voices. With the popularity of MTV, urban street culture has invaded the home, and audiences across America have been reconditioned to accept unconventional imagery and jarring, surrealistic story lines resulting from the emphasis on music rather than narrative.

The videocassette, however, is the greatest threat to all other visual entertainment media. Since 1978, network television audiences have steadily declined as the videocassette industry has grown to earn annually as much as cinema box offices. Videocassette recorders sell at a rate of almost one million a month and are found in roughly one-third of American homes. Video rental stores are as common as supermarkets. In addition to movies, there are cassettes for advisory personal improvement and entertaining, board games,

books (children's literature is particularly popular), and exercise such as the best-selling "Jane Fonda Workout" series. Though renting cassettes is still preferable to purchasing them for most VCR owners, the retail costs of videos are showing marked decreases as the market becomes flooded with new releases.

On the horizon is the threat of pay-per-view cable, which allows the viewer to request movies at specific times for small fees. While this may deter some video purchasers from buying cassettes, it is unlikely to greatly disturb the rental market. After all, even if people are not going to the movie theater, they will still have to get out of the house.

RADIO

With the onset of television, the death of radio was predicted. Ironically, radio is surviving better than the other broadcasting media. It has a history of flux and format change, but 1985 showed a 15 percent growth in the industry, and targeting the Young Urban Professional audience has revitalized advertising with big business. The greatest change in radio is that listeners now select stations rather than programs. Research is radio's barometer, and demographics determine format. Radio reaches into all aspects of American lifestyle; it participates in every waking hour of American lives. There is the wake-up clock radio, the kitchen radio for breakfast news, and the car radio for its largest audience, the commuter. Radio is heard in offices, elevators, waiting rooms, and lobbies and is transported to the beach and on joggers' daily workouts. In fact, radio's greatest strength in competing with other media is its portability.

During radio's golden age in the 1930s and 1940s, specific programs attracted devoted audiences. People tuned in to the

Keith Glasgow

Radio was threatened by the advent of television, but it survived in large part because of its portability and most recently, because of its satellite linkage. It reaches into everyone's lives, from the wake-up radio and the commuter car radio to the "boom boxes" carried on the street.

adventures of "The Shadow," "Superman," "The Lone Ranger," and "Search for Tomorrow." News was an on-the-spot commodity, as evidenced by a WOR reporter's description, in a voice racked with sobs, at the horror of the *Hindenburg* explosion. Radio was first in formulating exercise, health, and entertainment shows. But as TV emerged, radio adapted to the competition with format programming. The teen market was targeted for records played by disc jockeys; small specialized stations proliferated for farmers, ethnic, and religious groups; commuters became a captive audience. The 1950s brought rock 'n' roll to the Top-40 format, and the 1960s followed suit as radio provided an album-oriented audience, which tuned in to the new FM spectrum. Even though AM signals reached farther, FM caught on because it offered superior sound quality and stereo capability. FM was coined "progressive" programming and played sets of protest music by Joan Baez, Phil Ochs, and Country Joe and the Fish to devoted followers. By the 1970s, however, FM's progressive station success led to more advertising and that, in turn, changed format and values. Automated equipment also affected FM's sound, with prerecorded announcements of news, concerts, and interviews. AM, which had gone "all-talk" and "all-news," had developed advisory programs on sex and psychology. The format syndrome burgeoned.

Format radio is as diverse as Americans' interests. Top-40, for example, developed more music, less chatter. It ran songs together and played golden oldies. WABC, with disc jockey Dan Ingram, was the leader and was one of the most listened-to stations in the country. It was deposed by the disco format of WKTU, New York, which capitalized on the popularity of the film *Saturday Night Fever.* WABC followed other AM stations in going all-talk as "contemporary" programming emerged. "Easy listen-

ing" was developed as an alternative, with its supposedly unobtrusive, heavily string-orchestrated environmental sound. Country, classical, and jazz formats grew. Religious stations were revived from the 1920s because of Nashville's affinity for gospel. Game shows became radio's tune-in gimmick; KFRC San Francisco adopted the style for six hours of weekday programming. "Adult contemporary" provided all-talk and easy listening. It hit the commuter hour and built on the popularity of top-name personalities like Don Imus, Charles Osgood, Paul Harvey, John Gambling, and Bernard Meltzer. All-talk stations like WOR utilized the talk-show format with call-ins.

All of these formatting approachs notwithstanding, the popularity and longevity of the all-news format is still going strong. As proven by New York City's WINS, news is the mainstay of radio. The minidocumentary provides short reports on current topics ranging from inflation to cancer. Networks offer news services tailored to fit formats of contemporary, entertainment, FM, or information news sounds. During the day, radio has the largest news audience of all broadcasting media.

Noncommercial or "alternative" radio ranges from locally supported school stations to our National Public Radio (NPR) system, which transmits via satellite to a weekly average of between four and five million listeners. WNYC created innovative programs—Mayor Fiorello La Guardia read comics on the air during New York City's 1945 news strike—and was the first municipally supported station. It is now one of NPR's over 300 affiliate stations reaching across the United States and Puerto Rico.

Certain shows have been identified as landmarks in broadcasting history. NBC's "Monitor," for example, lasted nearly twenty years. Begun as one of the few network experiments, it provided one of the first cores of celebrated anchorpeople

covering sports, news, and interviews—it even offered comedy. Bernard Meltzer's "What's Your Problem?" offers advice on everything from finances to psychological and social problems with a sticky-sweet personal rapport between Meltzer and call-in listeners. "Rambling With Gambling," radio's longest-running show hosted by three generations of the Gambling family, provides a down-to-earth service program of news and human-interest stories. WNYC's "Prairie Home Companion," created and hosted by Garrison Keillor, is a weekly selection of traditional and contemporary music combined with humor and philosophy segments based on a fictional town called Lake Wobegon, Minnesota. American Public Radio is venturing into the much-ignored area of children's programming with "Kids America"—a call-in show originated on WNYC. National Public Radio has produced two award-winning news programs, "All Things Considered" and "Morning Edition." "All Things Considered," first heard on the air in 1971, is ninety minutes of newscasts that feature business and economic reports, human interest and art features, media reviews, and documentary features on diverse topics such as nuclear face-off in Europe and the effects of development on the Georgian Sea Islands. National Public Radio also presents original and radio-adapted drama on "NPR Playhouse," and "Enfoque Nacional," America's only national broadcast Spanish language radio newsmagazine.

Radio's future is more secure than that of television or film. The inevitable changes for radio are the realization of AM's stereo capability, legislation requiring that all radios be manufactured to receive AM and FM, satellites as the norm for broadcasting, an increasing number of stations on expanding spectrums, and formats becoming more specialized as demographics become much more specific.

Wolfman Jack was the quintessential disc jockey of rock and roll in the 1950s. He introduced new hits, made up lingo, and determined what was in or out. He embodied the essence of "cool."

Courtesy of Kennedy Galleries, New York

The progression of fine arts in America during the last century resembles the evolution of a chick pea into a redwood forest. American artists have blazed a meteoric trail from their early struggle to find a native aesthetic voice in the shadow of their European counterparts to today's convergence of fashion, commerce, culture, politics, self-expression, and social voice, which has created a vital American forum at the hub of the international art world. Contemporary fine art in America has become an artistic phenomenon embodying energy, expressive diversity, and broad public appeal. With almost Hollywood appeal, contemporary artists have captured public imagination and spirit, generating enormous mainstream excitement and au-

Painting the fields and rolling hills of the Midwest, regionalist artist Thomas Hart Benton urged American artists to paint subjects from the area of the country where they were born. Drawing on his own experience, Benton sought to create an epic style that would champion America's history.

dience involvement. Galleries are opening by the hundreds throughout the country, exhibiting every kind of art from almost every era: Dealers, collectors, corporations, and other art enthusiasts are spending thousands of dollars for paintings, sculptures, prints, drawings; and the artist is enjoying a status and influence that was unimaginable in esoteric circles before 1970. Contemporary fine art is beginning to be recognized for its role in the telling and shaping of American culture rather than in its traditional milieu as a private, incomprehensible language for aesthetes and intellectuals.

The various art movements prevalent today (such as Neo-Expressionism, Neo-Realism, Neo-Surrealism, New Wave, Post-

Pop, Appropriation, Graffiti, and others) grew out of an ongoing debate between artists, critics, and the art public. The pluralism evident in contemporary art has proven that no one social group or artistic movement has absolute influence over art. Before World War II, Paris was considered the mecca for visual artists. During the war, however, many avant-garde European artists and intellectuals fled from war-time oppression to New York City, where they formed a new aesthetic community that eventually provided the art world with a new focal point: These artists introduced the catalytic energy that shaped American painting and transformed it in the twentieth century. Unlike Europe, America lacked the cultural tradition and estab-

lished patronage from which a native aesthetic ideology and expression could evolve; serious support for the "frivolous pursuit of compositon and color" was scattered and American art was considered to be stylistically disjointed. The war's end, however, heralded an era in which America began to establish its artistic identity—one that eventually enlarged the vision and scope of art throughout the world.

The first American artists drew on indigenous subjects: the unique geography and people of a land full of a "revolutionary brand of new ideas." Two predominant schools of artistic thought developed and continue to evolve today. On the one hand is art that grounds itself in clarity and precision—the practical and literal repre-

This poetic landscape by Winslow Homer, left, tells of a simpler time, when America was an isolated rural society, and its artists were not yet searching for an international style.

Private Collection, Courtesy of Kennedy Galleries New York

sentation of everyday existence that strives to define the "self" in relation to the environment. American life, in the images of urban and rural scenes and landscapes, was painted by popular genre artists such as Thomas Hart Benton, Winslow Homer, Andrew Wyeth, Grant Wood, Edward Hopper, and Grandma Moses, and continues to

The use of stark, contrasting light and isolated forms and colors give Edward Hopper's City Roofs *an immediate sense of urban loneliness. Underlying his reference to American consciousness during the 1930s, however, is a theme of quiet dignity that characterizes the continuing stability of "everyday life."*

Photo Courtesy of Leo Castelli Gallery, New York

Giving iconic status to an object straight off the shelves of popular consumer culture, Andy Warhol's Campbell's Soup, right, *is a classic Pop art image. As flamboyant as his pictures of movie personalities, the artist,* below, *is the progenitor of a new generation of "art stars."*

Scott Heiser

be interpreted and painted by an entirely new generation of Landscape, Primitive, and Realist artists.

The second predominant school of art transcends the literal and reevaluates the symbolic metaphor and abstract principles from which movements like Cubism, Fauvism, and Surrealism evolved. Artists such as Georgia O'Keeffe, Jackson Pollock, and Robert Motherwell drew on the work of Cubists and Surrealists and reinterpreted these forms to create a distinctly American art. In the fifties, the revolutionary Pollock drew on psychological and spiritual consciousness as he helped set the groundwork for the Abstract Expressionist movement, which established American art as an undeniable force in the world. As it had been for the Surrealists, who found images in dream languages, the Abstract Expressionists explored the realms of the unconscious; they rid their art of representational images and left gestures of pure emotional energy. Georgia O'Keeffe, for example, transcended the literal with work imbued with quiet mystery as she expressed the sublime face of nature in her paintings of desert life. This new style of art dealt with ambiguous images that the viewer did not always understand, and it elicited fervent reactions from the art public. While many described abstraction as the wave of the future, others considered it to be too difficult to comprehend—claiming that its images were too elitest.

Indeed, "What is it; what does it mean?" are the primary questions in the ongoing dialogue between the audience, the critic, and the artist. At the inception of this "new" Modernism, the relatively isolated art-viewing American public was faced with a new aesthetic, one which exploded the boundaries of classical form and representational art; the Abstract Expressionists revealed the expressive possibilities of avant-garde thinking as it related to Ameri-

Photo Courtesy of Leo Castelli Gallery, New York

Reminiscent of his days as a billboard painter, James Rosenquist's bold, colorful style confronts the audience with an ironic allusion to America's budding advertising age with Growth Plan. *Modeling BVDs for assorted sizes and ages, a line of "boy statues" stands to reassure our materialistic society that there is a product to accompany life's every incremental step.*

can culture and its artistic sensibility.

However, no matter how "far out" the new abstraction seemed to the public and to the critics, almost no one was prepared for what the sixties would bring. Pop entered with a flamboyant, irreverent, ambitious, and outrageous bang. An artistic phenomenon, Pop was appealing to a public starved for familiar images after what many considered to be the unintelligible and aloof representations of Abstract Expressionism. With bemused detachment,

artists like Jasper Johns, Roy Lichtenstein, Andy Warhol, and James Rosenquist derived their work from popular culture, creating pictures of cola cans and movie stars, and automobiles with gleaming grills personified as larger-than-life humanoids.

Realists, such as Philip Pearlstein, Alfred Leslie, and Alex Katz, who disassociated themselves from the abstract and Pop movements, were also active during the fifties and sixties, working in an uncompromising figurative style, while Photo Realists

such as Chuck Close, Malcolm Morley, and Audrey Flack transformed photographic information into painted images.

With the seventies came an infusion of styles and movements that further defined the parameters of the art scene. Creating new standards and vitalizing old ones, Judy Chicago coordinated one of this century's most ambitious art projects: *The Dinner Party,* a tribute to 1,038 women whom the artist considered influential in world history. Reminiscent of the grand scale co-

Courtesy of Mary Boone Gallery

With what at first glance appears to be a ceremonial wedding procession, Eric Fischl paints an eerie flip-side version of a bride's most memorable day, above. Exposing the nature of opposites tugging in the mind of the "human animal," right, David Salle's split-panel treatment in this portrait of a woman sets up a revealing psychological dichotomy.

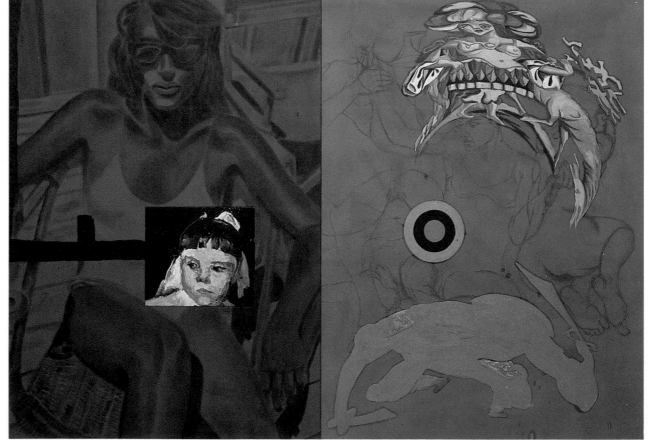

Photo Courtesy of Leo Castelli Gallery, New York

operatives of the old Master Renaissance studio project, Chicago's work was a unique mixture of mediums, tearing down some of the attitudinal barriers that separated the painted image from the crafted one. A multitude of seamstresses, china painters, ceramicists, artisans, and carpenters all combined their skills to create the multitextural quality of *The Dinner Party.* An early proponent of Pattern and Decorative art, Miriam Schapiro also helped break the rigid distinctions between the realms of high art and craft during the seventies. In her work she repeats motifs and designs that often are found in a rug or quilt; Schapiro infuses the designs with more than just a "superficial prettiness." With her decorative images, she explores and validates the "traditional" activities of women, connecting herself to the unknown quilters, the craft artists who did the invisible "woman's work."

American consciousness during the seventies was a strange mix of turbulence and emotional numbness resulting from the Vietnam War: The traditions of image-making were being challenged. Much of today's art is a reaction to the intellectual concerns of two of the art movements that developed during this period—Conceptualism, an art best described by the phrase "I think therefore I art" and the austere constraints of Minimalism, which dealt with the reduction of color, form, and image. Indeed, the highly acclaimed art object was quickly losing its position as an icon and it was taken to an extreme that nearly led to the complete eradication of form and image. Impermanent artwork such as Earth or Environmental Art, Performance Art, and Happenings turned creative expression into a transitory and immediate experience. To many, the seventies seemed to give rise to an unapproachably cerebral form of artistic expression.

While "high art" was at its apex, a storm was brewing in the studios of a new generation of artists who were searching for expressive alternatives to the forces that had shaped painting in the seventies. The result is evident in the amazing diversity of art today: Extreme opposites in style and method have confronted the cool detachment of the previous decade. An unapologetic eclecticism is creating exciting new possibilities in art. Indeed, one of the freedoms of this eclecticism is that the artist feels free to slip in and out of the portals of art history—reexamining that which has been to suit that which is. Also, more than at any other time in American history, art today is intertwined with the social and political nuances of our culture: Art invites the audience and the critics to challenge not only artistic preconceptions and standards, but also those of modern day dreams and apprehensions. The images explored by artists today, unlike the formalistically reverent ones of the seventies, are sometimes unsettling subjects that until now retained a "taboo" status. Some Realists working today (such as David Salle, Eric Fischl, and Jonathan Borofsky) recall early American scene painters in their representation of American life. However, much of what used to be depicted as "the American Dream" is reexamined today with a look at the seamier side of paradise, Mom, and apple pie. Eric Fischl imbues his work with sexual undertones as a means of exposing the flip side of an outwardly comfortable social order. He teases the viewer with discordant scenes of social transgressions that evoke sexual and psychic tension for the viewer.

Some of the most socially conscious art has emerged from very surprising sources—like inner city Graffiti Art. While contemporary artists are drawing upon the whole of art history, they are also utilizing the stimuli around them, and the urban landscape provides a powerful set of sym-

Paula Court

From the subway walls to gallery canvases to his own line of tee shirts, Keith Haring's caricatures of three-eyed video monsters and "radiating babies"—like the artist himself—are familiar sights in New York City.

Right: Creating an image that lives somewhere between graffiti writing and fetish carving, Jean-Michel Basquiat layers and scratches his paint on wood or canvas. After establishing his career in the fifties and sixties painting landscape and figure studies, Richard Diebenkorn is today one of America's most re-known artists. His masterful **Ocean Park Series,** *below, (begun in 1967) reflects the "light years" that American abstract painting has traveled since the thirties.*

Jean-Michel Basquiat

bols. It is possible to look to a concrete wall or a booth in a night club as well as to the wall of a museum for the pictures of life today—as disturbing or base as they may seem. Keith Haring and Jean-Michel Basquiat, who began their careers by drawing, scratching, and spray-painting subway stairwells and city sidewalks, represent the artist renegade who has literally come in from the dark to scribble his primal tatoos on artistically and publically sanctioned walls. Basquiat, along with Kenny Scharf and Rodney Alan Greenblat, reflects in his work a stylistic simplicity similar to that found in the motifs and colors of Primitive art. The work of these artists—however stylistically naive and deliberately "crude"—evokes a sense of a self-styled ritual born of street-wise savvy rather than one of quaint pastoral composure.

Drawing not only on Realist traditions and the freedoms made possible through abstraction, Neo-Expressionists such as Julian Schnabel, David Salle, Susan Rothenberg, Jonathan Borofsky, Eric Fischl, Judy Pfaff, Charles Clough, Frank Young, Louise Fishman, Bill Jensen, and others represent a new interpretive force in art today. The emotive power suggested by the use of strong primary colors, aggressive brushwork, and figural distortions in their work is challenging some accepted methods and standards. In one sense, the return to expressionistic art (whether figurative or abstract) is a radical act following the distrust of the art object and the reduction of color and pictorial space apparent in the seventies. Similar to stream-of-consciousness—with the image forming itself spontaneously from the manipulation of paint—Susan Rothenberg's horses are painted loosely and with a sense of unfettered movement and free association rather than with a strict or rigid formula. Evoking the metaphoric allusion to landscape with organic images and structured space, the work of Jed Gared and Andrea Chase is reminiscent of surrealistic dreamscapes—scenes that deal more with the panorama of the mind than of nature.

The barrage of mass media intruding on every aspect of our lives has never been more apparent. Everywhere audio-visual messages give us cues on how to lead the "good life." And once again, a generation of artists is making a visual investigation of how kitsch, advertising, television, and movies play on the perceptions and presentiments of society. Reminiscent of Pop art, artists such as Barbara Kruger, Cindy Sherman, Sherry Levine, and Mike Bidlo are producing psychologically and visually jolting images—offering pointed commentaries rather than just serving up deadpan satires. With her searing juxtapositions of simple images and blunt text, Barbara Kruger is one of the leading exponents of a contemporary photography that is grounded in the questionable ethics of mass communication and advertising. In one piece, she boldly prints the headline "WHAT BIG MUSCLES YOU HAVE" over a background of printed phrases of coy endearment meant to illustrate the things women "traditionally" say to men. Cindy Sherman's photographic self-portraits, in which she dresses herself up in an astounding array of guises and "self-conscious" psychic states, parodies the ef-

Courtesy of Metro Pictures, New York

Illuminated from behind with vivid dream-like color, a nameless figure peers ominously through a barrier of dried grasses in this Cindy Sherman self-portrait photograph. By creating a scene that intertwines the literal with the surreal, the artist entices her audience to "put their finger" on the character she portrays.

Right: *Creating his own "comic mythology," Rodney Alan Greenblat enshrines the relatives of Betty Boop and the Tin Man in this altar-like construction. Recalling the "down home" naïveté of Primitivist art, Greenblat presents his view of the world with animated satire—but with a more "worldly" punctuation. Experimenting with dimensionality thrice-removed, Charles Clough shuffles and reshuffles layers of sensuously emotive flowing color with homemade "painting fingers,"* below.

A commentary on the violence of street life, or of some kind of inner turbulence? Pushing beyond the rectangular boundaries of his canvases, Robert Longo portrays a cubed projectile and a flash of light in a freeze frame hovering beside an inverted painting of a man's face.

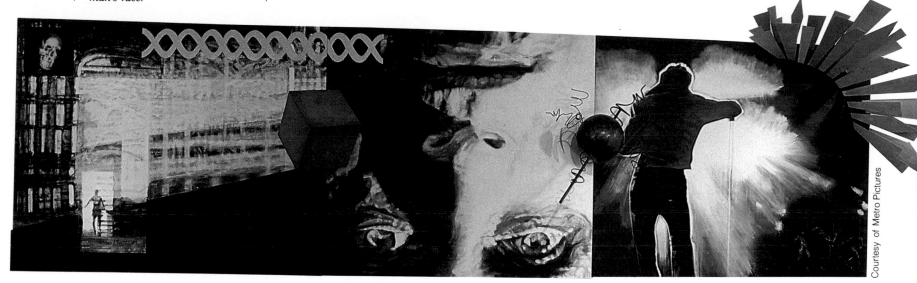

fects of multimedia radiation on "the girl next door." Suggesting that the concept of artistic originality is merely another media myth, Sherry Levine and Mike Bidlo literally copy or "appropriate" the works of other artists—showing them as their own—making it clear that piracy, along with its accompanying overtones of infringement and lack of privacy, is exactly the point.

Some critics see Appropriation, which completely shatters the "hallowed principles of original expression" and ideals of what art should be, as "true" Postmodern art. Alex Katz translates the ordinary sights of day-to-day life into images that are of personal import—his family, his dog, his neighbors—and transforms them into images that have a broader cultural meaning. His images capture the eye with the use of flashy color on a grand scale that is reminiscent of billboards, fashion, and movies. Using similar materials, Ed Paschke selects photographs of public figures that are then collaged, overpainted, and projected onto a canvas. The resulting images abandon the quest for a perfect likeness, and instead depict a kind of visual mythology.

Numerous other "isms" and "neos" are being formed in paint and plaster as the spectrum of cultural experience shifts: Since the fifties, American art has recorded the enormous societal changes that have taken place. It has been said that art imitates life, and the role of the artist is more than that of keeping track of individual creative stirrings: The artist provides a visual "conscience of race." And today's American artists are delivering some pointed observations. Many critics feel that contemporary art relies too heavily on attention-grabbing shock tactics that deliberately deprive the public of the pleasing gratifications that a "prettier picture" might afford. In this dialogue between artist and critic lies one key to how fine art in America has progressed in this century and to how the public has reacted. More and more people are relying on creative solutions to their modern-day concerns; they are discovering that art does indeed reflect the consciousness of the times. While searching for individual truths, the artist holds up to society its own mirror image—painting a timeless "portrait" that serves to confront and enlighten. In this role, the artist in America is no longer labeled a wayward explorer of the esoteric out-of-bounds, but a creative scientist, observer, politician, social commentator, entrepreneur, and most of all, teacher.

THE PRINTED WORD

Gayle Jann

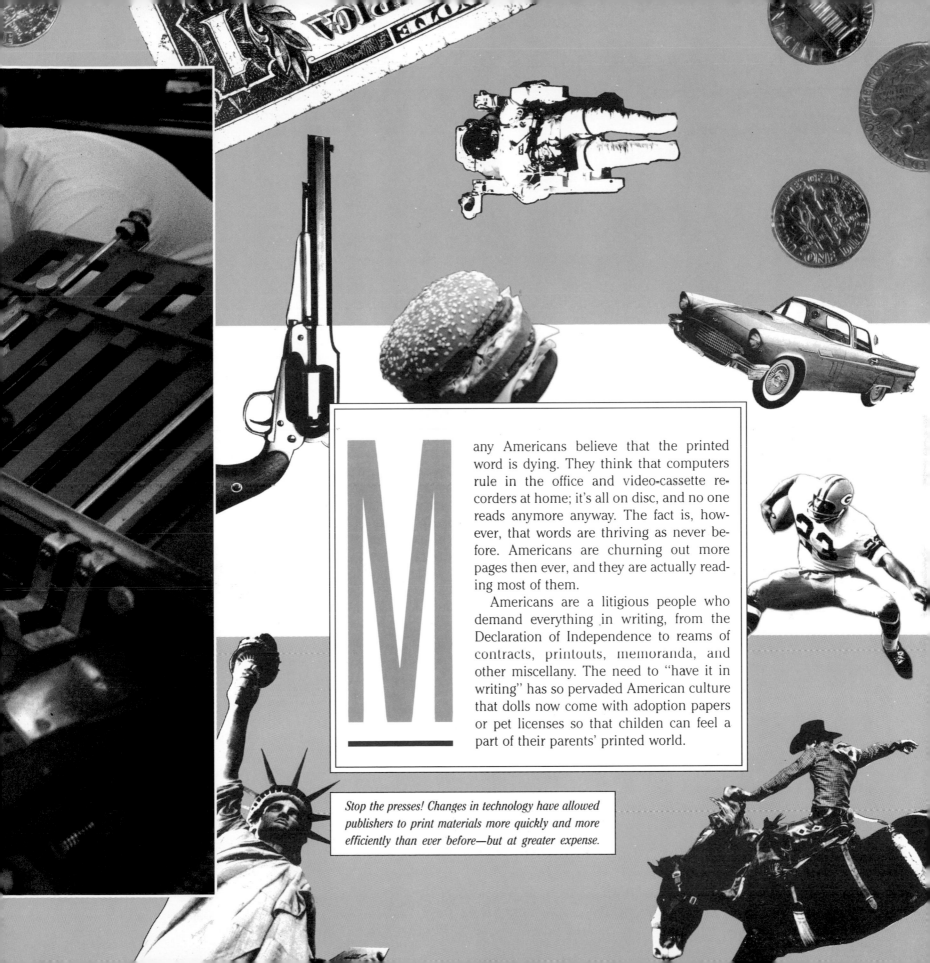

Many Americans believe that the printed word is dying. They think that computers rule in the office and video-cassette recorders at home; it's all on disc, and no one reads anymore anyway. The fact is, however, that words are thriving as never before. Americans are churning out more pages then ever, and they are actually reading most of them.

Americans are a litigious people who demand everything in writing, from the Declaration of Independence to reams of contracts, printouts, memoranda, and other miscellany. The need to "have it in writing" has so pervaded American culture that dolls now come with adoption papers or pet licenses so that childen can feel a part of their parents' printed world.

Stop the presses! Changes in technology have allowed publishers to print materials more quickly and more efficiently than ever before—but at greater expense.

USA Today *offers the news in a fast-food format that has led to its being affectionately nicknamed "McPaper."*

Despite blatant shortcomings in the education of many segments of the population, more Americans are reading than ever before. Of course, there are more Americans than ever before as well. But the requirement of functional literacy for gainful employment and everyday survival increases steadily. While printed words are usually associated with bound books and daily newspapers, they continue to assault most Americans in countless other ways. Billboards, posters, brochures, programs, bills, and reports use them in growing numbers. Much of this is due to technology and the growing availability of computers/printers, photocopiers, and inexpensive presses.

American advances in technology have led directly to the rapid expansion of one particularly American printed form—the newsletter. In its usual format as a subscription publication, a newsletter's purpose is to offer specialized information in direct, accessible language to a targeted readership. That information may be insider news, industry gossip, government statistics, club calendars, alumni updates, how-to explanations, personal predictions, or hard-news reporting.

In its many forms, the newsletter may well be the most prevalent form of printed publication in the United States and the world. For most, "production" is simply copying, mimeographing, or small-time printing. Newsletters require little investment capital, don't pander to advertisers (they usually do not carry ads), and can be distributed quickly. A recent introduction in the field has been the computerized newsletter, available to personal computers through the growing number of consumer-information services. These newsletters can be updated at the touch of a keyboard and are usually available with an entire "menu" of other services. As the number of people using personal computers at home and in the office grows, computer newsletters will soon occupy a sizable percentage of the newsletter market.

The oldest continually published newsletter in this country is *The Kiplinger Washington Letter,* a comparatively generalized update on national political and economic concerns. Until 1982, it had been the largest circulation newsletter in the country, but was then eclipsed by *The Contest News Letter* (for coupon-clippers and Grand Prize-seekers). The nature of newsletters is so diverse that one financial newsletter is required to report on the accuracy of other financial newsletters (and will there one day be a newsletter to rate the rating newsletters?). For a nominal yearly fee, you can get *Bondage Quarterly* (relax, it's the official newsletter for the James Bond 007 Fan Club), and for two hundred times that fee John Oliphant, a Washington insider, will fill you in on the energy world. Major industries are the subject of scores of newsletters, whose efficacy is questioned by some. Whether insider tips will earn back the hundreds (if not thousands) of dollars it costs the readers each year to subscribe is uncertain, but as long as company presidents and CEOs believe so, newsletters of that nature will continue to exist.

There may not be as many newspapers as there are newsletters, but newspapers' circulations and cumulative pages represent the most extensive use of the printed word in America. Despite the growth of television news coverage, the percentage of the adult population that reads newspapers hasn't changed since the early 1970s. Two-thirds of all adults will look at a paper on any given weekday. Whether it's the sports pages, comics, gossip columns, coupons, or actual news, Americans continue to rely on newspapers for a great deal of information and entertainment.

While readership has remained strong, however, the number of daily newspapers has been slowly decreasing. These days, very few new papers are being introduced. And with more expensive technology being developed yearly, those papers on the fringe of survival find themselves capitulating. Large city papers are edging out suburban products from circulation, and rural mergers continue to decrease the total number of papers each year.

Surprisingly, researchers find that the growth of *USA Today,* the first "national" newspaper, has not had much effect on the circulation of local papers. For most of its readers, *USA Today* is a supplement to their local papers or a traveler's way of learning about other parts of the country.

While *USA Today* may have left local papers' finances intact, its effect on their editorial content has bothered many in the field. Soon after its inception, *USA Today* became known as "McPaper," implying a fast-food, processed version of reporting. An early *Time* magazine article put it this way: "Like local newscasts, *USA Today* stresses human interest and the pocket-book impact of events." In addition, the paper has spurred the use of color photographs and eye-catching charts and graphs. On slow news days, feature headlines may report national opinion polls or catchy patriotic homilies.

"McPaper" is owned by the Gannett Newspaper Syndicate, which owns over one hundred other papers as well. Gannett is, according to the same *Time* article, hoping "that *USA Today* will become the definitive newspaper of the television generation." It is, in fact, that generation that has positioned *USA Today* alongside The *Wall Street Journal* and New York's *Daily News* as a best-selling newspaper. However, while *USA Today*'s circulation has grown as well as Gannett Chairman Allen Neuharth could have hoped for, its financial situation has been nowhere near as positive. The massive network necessary to create, produce, and distribute a national daily has proved costly, and advertising remains an uphill battle. Traditionally, newspaper advertisers are local concerns, addressing themselves to a targetable audience. *USA Today,* instead, must convince advertisers to put their magazine-style na-

Robert Landau

| *Regional papers continue to cover certain events neglected in national publications.* |

tional campaigns into newsprint. Their success, or lack thereof, will greatly influence whether future attempts are made at creating other national papers.

The mere concept of a *USA Today* would be a pipe dream without the newspaper and magazine industries' position on the cutting edge of technology. In progressing from movable type to electronic transmission, their ability to produce the printed word is similar to radio's evolution from vacuum tube to transistor. Computerized layouts and satellite relays allow national magazines to reach the newsstand in as little as twenty hours after the events they are covering. (See page 117.) And the newspaper industry has proved to be a pioneer in relating the effects of improved technology on the workforce—the Rand Corporation reports that the newspaper industry is showing other industries what to expect for themselves and their employees.

Far less on the cutting edge of technology—somewhere in between newspapers and magazines—lie the weekly tabloids. The format encompasses everything

from gossip rags to chronicles of the avantgarde. Most major American cities can claim an arts-oriented weekly in print, with varying amounts of investigative journalism, concert listings, advertisements, and amorous personals. Boston's *Phoenix* and Minneapolis' *City Pages* are two good examples of well-written and interestingly addressed arts weeklies.

In almost complete contrast to these papers are the sensationalist tabloids sold in almost every supermarket in the country. From a TV queen's secret affair to the lastest photos of Siamese twin snakes, these weeklies are fascinating reflections of the culture they appeal to. They are recession-proof wonders that rely on newsstand sales in the millions instead of advertising revenues. Magazines such as *Time* or *People* get 60 percent of their income from advertising, while the *National Enquirer's* ad income accounts for only 12 percent of its total sales. And the kind of advertising that does appear in weeklies is very different from that of most other publications; there are miraculous grapefruit-diet plans,

The New Yorker, *despite its recent emphasis on increased advertising revenues, remains a symbol of editorial independence and—to some—literary excellence.*

before-and-after testimonies for bust enlargers, guaranteed mail-order diamond jewelry, and a cornucopia of weird and usually inexpensive items.

Anomalies in the field of weeklies, tabloids have little in common with most magazines. Magazine publishing has become an increasingly lucrative field, where fewer individuals and companies are coming to own a greater percentage of major national magazines. "Merger mania" was rampant in the mid-eighties, when sky-high price tags made it possible for just a small number of people to pursue titles. Media baron Rupert Murdoch was one who could afford those price tags. After acquiring a number of big-city daily papers, including the *New York Post* and *Chicago Sun-Times,* Murdoch turned to magazines. Known for a brand of journalism that has been described as "frequently pugnacious, sensational, and strident," Murdoch's Australian-based News Corporation has obtained such diverse and highly visible publications as *New Woman* and *The Star*, as well as a humorously opposite pair of New York City weeklies. Shortly after purchasing the ultra-Yuppie, status-conscious *New York* magazine, Murdoch bought *The Village Voice*—once a relatively radical politics and arts magazine, now a publication advertised on local TV for its eclectic personals and apartment listings complete with floor-plan maps. He has since sold *The Voice* and used the money to purchase several TV networks, a more-pervasive and powerful medium.

Murdoch's brightest score, however, was part of the biggest magazine deal of all. When the Ziff-Davis Company announced the sale of twenty-four of its titles, Murdoch was able to make off with half of them. CBS Publishing bought the other half, and in doing so immediately transformed itself from an also-ran publisher into one of the biggest. The combined sales netted William Ziff more than seven hundred million dollars, though he refused at the time to discuss why he was choosing to disband an empire it had taken him a lifetime to create. Nonetheless, Ziff retained eleven computer magazines.

The outcome, unfortunately, was still another consolidation of magazine ownership. One media expert has warned that "we now have a small group of owners with remarkably similar political and social views. As a result, our major media probably offer the narrowest range of ideas available in any developed democracy." The argument may be a bit overstated, but a look at other multimagazine owners shows a sameness in attitude and outlook that can be scary. The Condé Nast Group of magazines, owned by S.I. Newhouse; who also owns the *New Yorker* (a symbol of editorial independence), are based on such a white, upper-class, beautiful-people ideal that they "are virtual clones in terms of their upscale ambience, their upbeat tone, and their materialistic philosophy."

These days, the ownership of a major newsmagazine, network, or newspaper has become increasingly valuable. The ability to report about, partake in, and occasionally have an effect upon global events is a powerful asset. Ted Turner, Rupert Murdoch, and others have thrust themselves into positions of visible power through their ownership of such outlets. In a recent article on the sale of *U.S. News & World Report,* a magazine consultant wrote: "After all, there are only three newsmagazines —and there may never be another chance to buy one of them. Their influence is enormous, the publisher is privy to the inner workings of virtually everything everywhere, and he can get an audience with anyone in the world, at any time, if he wants." It helps that the magazines are also increasingly profitable.

Regional magazines have also found

great success in recent years. Covering business, arts and entertainment, politics, trends, and other localized special interests, these magazines thrive because they appeal to both readers and advertisers. The number of area business publications such as *Manhattan, Inc.* have increased five-fold during the eighties, helping corporate movers and shakers keep up on one another. Major cities like New York, Washington, and Los Angeles are the subject of glossy, high-quality magazines, while scores of smaller cities (and/or states) feature monthlies and quarterlies of varying sophistication. For upscale, urban newcomers, as well as third-generation natives, regional publications have become a popular alternative and/or supplement to national magazines with a broader focus.

The staggering diversity of monthlies, quarterlies, and journals continues to expand, and it is the independently produced periodicals that are providing some of the most thought-provoking material available in any printed form. From the floor-coverings industry to rock 'n' roll fanzines, low-circulation periodicals are available on hundreds of subjects. Every trade and industry has at least one (unless they've just got newsletters!) and then there are those for hobbyists, athletes, political groups, parents, record collectors, history buffs, etc., etc., etc. Literary journals like *The Sewanee Review* and *Grand Street* battle financial pressures and still manage to compile superb issues. The number of fascinating, captivating small publications certainly exceeds the number of trashy ones. Even if names like *Worldview, Parabola,* and *Landscape* aren't quite as well-known as *People* or *Family Circle,* they are still first-rate vehicles for the printed word.

Similar to the magazine industry, book publishers—nearly twenty thousand in number—are a very diverse lot, with a vast array of specialties and interests. Also like magazines, major book publishing companies are emerging from a series of takeovers and mergers that has reshaped the business. In some cases, larger houses have purchased smaller ones, consolidating into more powerful entities. Others have been absorbed themselves by enormous conglomerates. G.P. Putnam's Sons, one of the oldest houses, was purchased by MCA, better known for its movies and records. While a publishing company like Putnam's might lose much of its independence, it suddenly gains access to valuable titles as well. While MCA's film division was raking in box-office receipts for the movie *E.T.,* its book and record holdings were developing tie-in projects. Putnam's eventually would release novelizations and storybook versions that would be translated into every major language in the world, including Russian. (It should be noted that another publishing house, Simon & Schuster, would be granted the rights to release about a dozen children's titles based on *E.T.,* including coloring books and educational-activity books. Ownership by such a conglomerate does not guarantee tie-in rights, but it can't hurt.)

The inordinate profits available from one single title has helped create a blockbuster mentality in the major houses. In addition to film tie-ins, *Iacocca* and other "how-I-made-it" biographies have helped direct the publishing industry's attention to nonreaders. While attempts are being made to help the twenty-five million functionally illiterate adults in this country, there is a related problem that is just as severe and, some believe, harder to treat. Aliterates are people who *can* read, but don't. Over half of the American public has not read a single book in the last six months, and the reading of books is on the decline among sixteen- to twenty-one-year-olds. As a result, the book publishing industry is realizing that it must sell the idea of reading to Americans before

Susan M. Duane

As chain stores give more and more space to calendars, tapes, and other non-book products, book lovers are finding other places to satisfy their reading needs.

In the war for readers, newspapers have returned to the streets, replacing "read all about it" paperboys with vending machines.

Susan M. Duane

it can sell them books.

Consequently, original fiction is becoming an actual burden to many publishers, particularly works by first-time authors. Many small presses have taken on fledgling novelists, and these lesser-known houses are rapidly becoming a farm system for the larger ones.

Fiction, despite the dwindling space reserved for it on bookstore shelves, remains the most analyzed and discussed form of writing. A number of critical circles exist in America, with respective favorites and outcasts rarely corresponding. As soon as more than two or three young talents display something in common, a "movement" is declared. Bobbie Ann Mason and Ellen Gilchrist are among a number of young Southern females responsible for that group's rise in prominence. And, as always, there exists a group of veteran novelists for whom every publication marks an important event. While Joyce Carol Oates continues to increase her already-enormous oeuvre, the recent works of John Updike, E.L. Doctorow, Kurt Vonnegut, and others

have attracted great attention.

The combination of limited shelf space and veteran favorites make breaking in difficult. This applies to the smaller presses as well as the unknown author. And as chain stores, such as B. Dalton's or Waldenbooks, replace the remaining local, independent stores, distribution is more easily monopolized. The limited shelf space is also partially due to the growth of audio publishing and its place in the market. Some companies in the field seem to see a future where reading will give way to listening in the same way that analog watches have to digital, or shoelaces to Velcro, but for now that seems unlikely.

An area that should have a more immediate effect on how we view books is that of computers. From the method by which they are produced to the way we hold and use them, computers will change the way we obtain and read the printed word. Regardless, the spirit of the word and the information it carries should remain familiar for a long time to come. Novels written for and on the computer may introduce

new avenues of fiction, changes in structure, or the incorporation of moving type or special graphics. Perhaps in its early, gimmicky, experimental stages, the computer novel will give us concrete poetry in a mobile form or rumbling type for earthquake stories (like a cheap "sensurround" disaster movie). Where it goes from there is in the hands of the authors-programmers of the future.

As the means of self-expression become more varied, so too will the messages they convey. An emphasis on financial concerns at the commercial level has actually been helpful in creating a grass-roots movement in the world of fiction. It has been a while since a major stylistic movement affected the fiction scene, but it may be that present conditions are in the process of generating the next one. The printed word itself is as strong as ever, but it's what is done with it that counts. While it continues to be used to appeal to our basest instincts, the printed word remains capable of chronicling Americans at, and inspiring them to, their very best.

The best illustration of the incredible advancements in publishing technology is the state-of-the-art system currently in use at Time Inc. The Atex system allows *Time*'s correspondents, editors, researchers, and production people access to stories at the touch of a keyboard. And then the Crossfield system takes over with hookups to the printing plants, where it is possible to revise stories *between* printings. To illustrate the incredible rapidity of *Time*'s publication process, below is a chronological breakdown of one of its most remarkable feats; its coverage of President Reagan's controversial visit to the Bitburg cemetery on May 6, 1985. (All times are for the New York headquarters.)

5:40 A.M./Sunday: Reagan visits cemetery, lays wreath at memorial. By this time much of the story has already been written, and the space reserved for additional copy and photographs.

7:30 A.M./Sunday: Photos of the event have already been flown to *Time*'s Hanover, Germany photolabs and are being developed.

8:30 A.M./Sunday: Photos are selected for the cover and article, and put aboard a chartered plane for *Time*'s Holland offices, where a photolink facility will send them to New York. By this time, any update in copy has been made and sent by normal phonelines to the New York offices for incorporation into the article.

1:40 P.M./Sunday: Photos have arrived in Holland where the engraving process that prepares them for the printing process is begun. By 4:15, digitized four-color photos have been transmitted back to New York and are being programmed into the layouts.

3:00 P.M./Sunday: Final editorial revisions are made on the story.

6:00 P.M./Sunday: All information has been sent to the printing plants (nine in the United States, an additional nine throughout the world for international editions), which have already prepared the rest of the magazine. Within twelve hours, the story of Reagan's visit is actually coming off the presses.

2:00 A.M./Monday: The print run for the issue, some 5,200,000 copies, is completed. Issues are then packaged by *Time* for distribution to newsstands and post offices across the country.

7:00 A.M./Monday: Barely twenty-four hours after the event, copies of the issue have arrived in New York, Washington, D.C., Philadelphia, Chicago, and Los Angeles. There are copies in the Senate and other key government offices.

9:00 A.M./Monday: As people hurry to work, *Time* magazine is available on their newsstands, the morning after the event. Most home subscribers will receive their copies the next day, Tuesday, which is when some local papers will first be providing similar information.

CHAPTER

11 ★ SPORTS

John McDonough

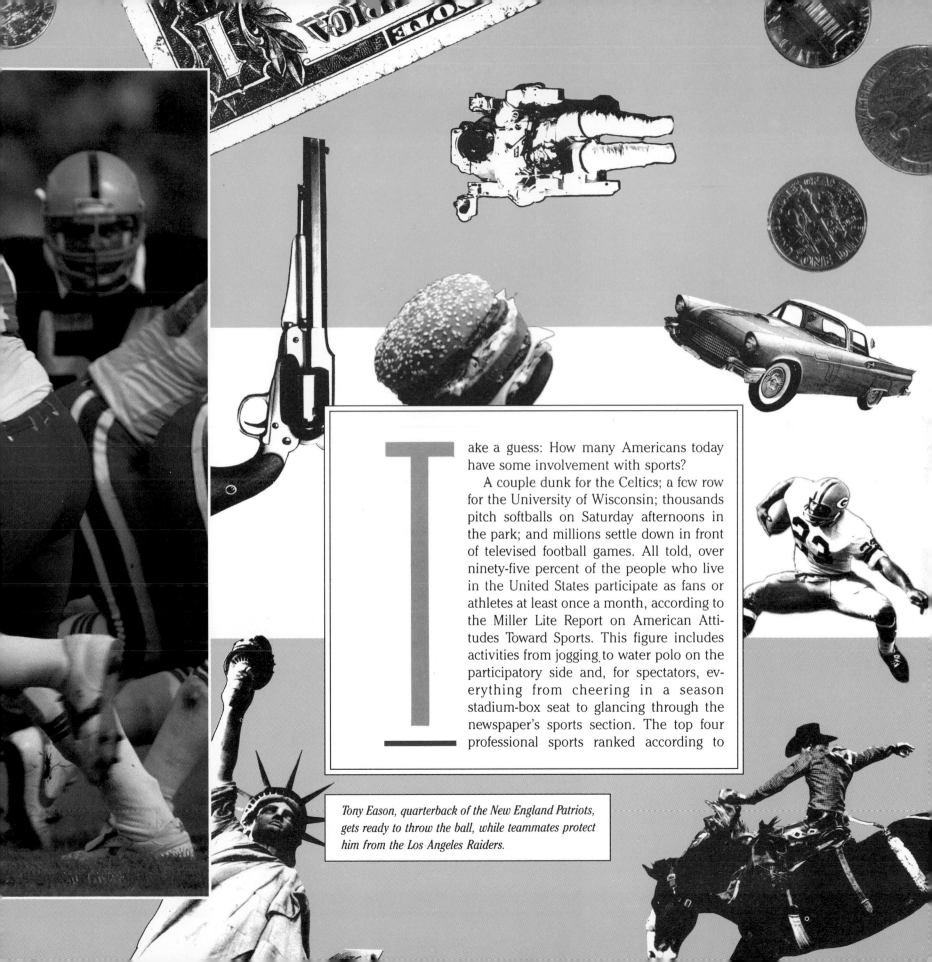

ake a guess: How many Americans today have some involvement with sports?

A couple dunk for the Celtics; a few row for the University of Wisconsin; thousands pitch softballs on Saturday afternoons in the park; and millions settle down in front of televised football games. All told, over ninety-five percent of the people who live in the United States participate as fans or athletes at least once a month, according to the Miller Lite Report on American Attitudes Toward Sports. This figure includes activities from jogging to water polo on the participatory side and, for spectators, everything from cheering in a season stadium-box seat to glancing through the newspaper's sports section. The top four professional sports ranked according to

Tony Eason, quarterback of the New England Patriots, gets ready to throw the ball, while teammates protect him from the Los Angeles Raiders.

spectator popularity are football, baseball, basketball, and hockey, and the most popular participatory sports are swimming, bicycling, jogging, and calisthenics.

Sports Affect Education, Politics, the Economy, and the Media

Physical education is mandatory in America's public schools. However, parental guidance in competitive games is just as important to a child's development as a teacher's instruction. Even before entering the first grade, most children have absorbed rules of sportsmanship from adults. Statistics show that three out of four Americans believe athletes are good role models for children.

Outside of school, competition under adult supervision is available in numerous youth leagues, the largest of which are Little League baseball (2.5 million participants) and Pop Warner football (250,000 participants). Criticism that some parents try to fulfill personal ambitions through their children may have tempered wholehearted support of these leagues, but opportunities for fun and growth usually outweigh most opposition.

Over half of all American children continue athletic competition after a grammar school introduction, competing in high school, college, an amateur or professional league, or the Olympics, according to the survey by Miller Lite. The majority who do not become professional athletes still have gained a valuable lesson: self-discipline.

Keith Glasgow

ARMCHAIR ATHLETES

34 percent of those Americans who participate in a sport daydream about athletic success. 45 percent believe they could do as well as a famous athlete if they had the same training, 30 percent believe they have better judgment than a coach, and 45 percent believe they could officiate more carefully than a referee or umpire.

—from the Miller Lite Report

Many children are introduced to organized competition through junior league soccer, left. *Cyclists round a curve at high speed,* right, *during the cycling finals of the 1984 Olympics.*

Gymnastics has become more popular than ever since the likes of Mitch Gaylord captured America's eye in the 1984 Olympic Games. A contemporary American youth is just as likely to go to a Saturday morning gymnastics workout as to a sandlot baseball game or a touch football game.

WHEN THE GAME IS OVER, THEN WHAT?

The following are several American public figures who first made their mark as athletes:

In 1937, Byron "Whizzer" White was the National Collegiate Athletic Association (NCAA) top student/football player in the categories of rushing and scoring. Since then, he has become a justice on the Supreme Court. Jack Kemp, former Buffalo Bills quarterback, is a nationally recognized political figure.

The person who holds the Ivy League record for highest basketball scorer is Princeton alumnus Bill Bradley, who later played for the New York Knicks and then became a New Jersey senator.

Ed Marinaro, famous as Officer Joe Coffey on TV's "Hill Street Blues," was a well-known running back for the Minnesota Vikings.

The influence politics has on sports is evidenced by more than just the political aspirations of some athletes. Recognizing that competition evokes patriotism, a politician might ally himself with a basketball team, trying to extend fan support of the team to himself. When the United States government boycotts the Olympic Games, it is using its athletes, men and women who probably do not want politics linked with their activity, to make a political statement. Incidents such as these cause some Americans to question whether political considerations have overstepped boundaries in influencing sports.

Millions of dollars are tied to the business of sports. When a major league baseball strike occurs, not only do fans, players, and owners lose, but advertisers and marketers are affected, as well as television, radio, and the print media. TV advertisers pay more than one million dollars for a commercial minute during the Super Bowl (the National Football League's championship game), compared to an average cost of two hundred thousand dollars per minute during prime time or thirty thousand dollars per minute during daytime, according to "ADWEEK's Marketer's Guide to Media."

Companies cash in on America's preoccupation with sports figures by presenting them as endorsers, presuming that Americans will buy the products they see their heroes using. Sometimes the endorsement is credible, as when Magic Johnson (the Los Angeles Laker's basketball player) jumps in a certain pair of sneaker's. However, when Dan Marino (the Miami Dolphins' quarterback) and Joe Montana (the San Francisco 49ers' quarterback) plug diet soda, one understands that money is the lure, not product suitability.

Often times, large companies promote goodwill by sponsoring athletic events. Examples include the prestigious Virginia Slims tennis tournament, and the Mobil TAC/USA Indoor Track and Field Championships. Most large athletic events would not happen without the generous dollar support of corporate sponsors.

While other runners set their watches just before the L'Eggs Mini Marathon in New York City, the concentration of number one ranked Grete Waitz turns inward for reflection.

Gayle Jann

Steve Smith/Wheeler Pictures

Swimmers shoot from the starting blocks during 1983 pre-Olympic practice in Los Angeles.

WOMEN AND SPORTS

The 1970s saw a burst of athletic activity from American women. Although great American female athletes had broken through social barriers in the past (Babe Didrikson, for example, in the 1930s excelled in track-and-field events, basketball, and golf), it took government support and a fiery women's rights movement to change attitudes toward women's competition. When Title IX of the Educational Amendment Acts of 1972 was passed, school and college sports programs for men and women had to be equally funded. Women took advantage of the new law, and from 1970 to 1980 the number of high school female athletes jumped from 294,000 to nearly 2 million. Consequently, the number of women participating as athletes and fans after the school years has increased.

Equal opportunity in sports has brought dramatic record-breaking as well; marathon running is a striking example. In 1983, two Americans held world records for the marathon—Alberto Salazar at 2:08:13 and Joan Benoit at 2:22:43. Compare these times to 1969 records, when Australian Derek Clayton was the fastest male marathoner at 2:08:33.6, and West German Anni Pede-Erdkant held the women's record, at 3:07:26. In fourteen years, the men's record was bettered by twenty seconds, while the women's record dropped nearly three-quarters of an hour.

Because of physical differences, women do not compete against men in sports where strength is a factor. However, female athletes are respected as much as males. Runner Mary Decker-Slaney and gymnast Mary Lou Retton are inspirational examples.

In the early twentieth century, *Jim Thorpe,* below, *described by some as the country's greatest athlete, excelled in football, as well as other sports. Joe Montana, number 16 of the San Francisco 49ers,* right, *is about to pass, as other 49ers block the defense.*

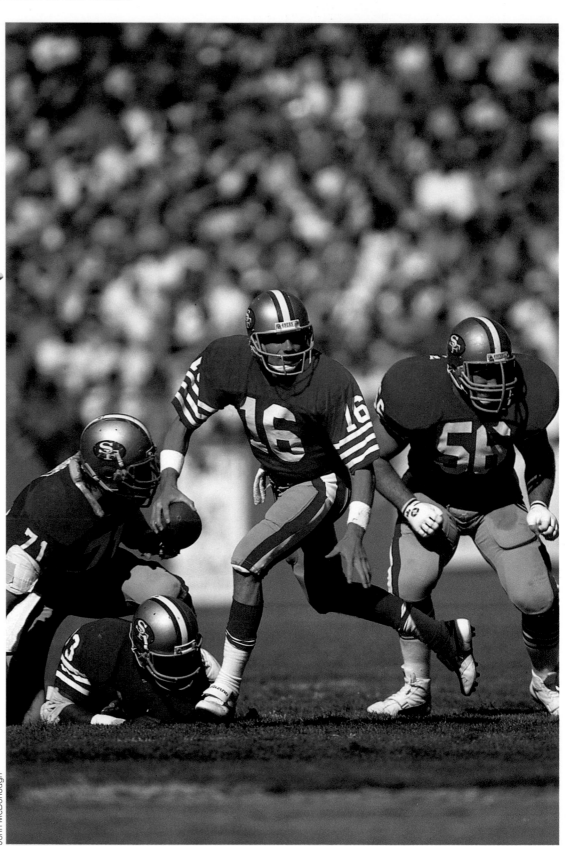

Library of Congress

John McDonough

America's enthusiasm for baseball hasn't changed much since the first game was played on Doubleday Field in Cooperstown, New York. Pictured here, two old rivals shake hands after a good game.

In the spring of 1983, Carl Lewis jumps long and longer, on his way to 1984's Olympic gold.

John McDonough

Library of Congress

Journalism has had a major impact on American sports, shaping the public's perception of athletes and often determining the commercial success of a professional team by print and broadcast coverage. Conversely, sports have transformed the media. As sportswriter Leonard Koppett noted, scores sell newspapers and newspapers give free publicity to sports events.

American television has helped enormously to expand the audience for professional sports by enabling people miles away from any sports team to root for a favorite. In the 1950s, when television-watching had become a favorite leisure activity, professional sports were marketed with more of a slant toward broadcast rather than live viewing, partly because replays and slow motion allow greater understanding of the game. More important perhaps, television brought greater revenue to the teams, exemplified by the National Football League's rise in income: less than fifteen million dollars per year in the sixties to a 2.1 billion dollar five-year, three-network contract in the eighties.

TV has also somewhat impeded the growth of sports in America by partly determining where sports franchises can be placed profitably, according to cities classed as major television markets. The three television networks, ABC, CBS, and NBC, program over twelve hundred hours of sports events every year. Sports and entertainment packager Don Ohlmeyer said, "I think we have a responsibility to not only put on what's popular, but to expose sports to the audience."

In 1979, the Entertainment Sports Programming Network (ESPN) gambled that America was sports-crazy enough to appreciate a twenty-four-hour sports-only cable channel. The gamble paid off, and today ESPN is well-established. However, overexposure can destroy a sport. Ohlmeyer gave the drop in the boxing audience in the 1950s as an example of TV overexposure.

Football has the greatest fandom of any professional sport in America. Some critics maintain that this is due to the fans' love of violence and the uninhibited release of tension that cheering play-warfare affords. Some say football's popularity is analogous to the growth of the white-collar population; indeed, a high percentage of football fans are well-educated and well-paid in professional jobs. A third explanation is that "less is more"; football teams play once a week, far less frequently than other top professional sports.

Television may be the biggest contributor to football's success, though, because broadcast coverage allows even a novice fan to understand the complex plays. Unlike hockey or baseball, where one should keep an eye on the entire playing area to appreciate the game (in baseball, for instance, you need to see the pitcher winding up and throwing, the runner on base leading off, the outfielder catching, etc.), football action occurs in one small part of the field that the cameras can focus on.

One of the hottest football players is Walter Payton, a Chicago Bear who started his NFL career in 1974 with the same team. Payton will probably be the first man to rush for more than one thousand yards in nine seasons. He broke Jim Brown's nineteen-year-old rushing record, and he also holds the record for combined yards gained and the most one hundred yard games in a career.

Baseball is called America's national pastime. Since 1910, the president of the United States has thrown out the first ball of the season, signaling for many the return of spring. Some describe baseball as a sport appealing to an older generation of America, a more leisurely paced way of play and way of life. That may be true, but consider this: When a baseball travels the sixty feet, six inches from the pitcher's hand to home

Los Angeles Ram Dieter Brock, number 5, has his eye on a fellow Ram to receive the ball.

John McDonough

In football, more than in any other game, cheerleaders heighten the excitement of an already action-packed competition, above.

John McDonough

Pete Rose, left, *of the Cincinnati Reds, is a record-holding player who has turned his skills to managing and has turned his team around. Nothing beats the excitement of a capacity crowd in Dodgers Stadium in Los Angeles,* below.

Keith Glasgow

plate at eighty-five miles per hour, the batter has about forty-five one hundreths of a second to decide whether or not to swing. Still think baseball is a slow game?

The baseball season lasts from April to October, culminating in the World Series, the best-of-seven-game tournament between the two top-league teams. The New York Yankees have won a record twenty World Series. Other notable records include Hank Aaron's 755 home runs, set in 1976, and Lou Gehrig's 2,130 consecutive games played, set in 1938. The closest a major league baseball player has come to Gehrig's record is when Steve Garvey played his 1,207th game in 1983, but then missed a possible 1,208th.

In 1927, Babe Ruth hit sixty home runs, surpassing the previous home-run-per-year record by nearly 150 percent and setting a record that he held for thirty-four years. The current home-run-per-year record stands at sixty-one, set by Roger Maris.

Pete Rose, player/manager of the Cincinnati Reds, is another one of baseball's hottest stars. He has played five different positions in sixteen All-Star games. Among other records, he owns the record for most base hits, breaking Ty Cobb's fifty-seven-year-old record of 4,191 in 1985. In the same year, his rookie season as a manager, he motivated the Reds to rise from the bottom of the barrel to second place in the National League's Western division.

Basketball was invented in 1891 so that fans would have something to cheer for between the baseball and football seasons. Since 1949, the National Basketball Association has regulated play of over twenty professional teams. Winners of the Eastern and Western Conference playoffs compete in May for the best of seven games.

An exemplary professional basketball career belongs to Wilt Chamberlain, who played for thirteen years. In 1962, he scored an average of 50.4 points per game,

Baseball entertains people of all ages. Here, a Dodgers fan enjoys lunch during the show.

Keith Glasgow

breaking the previous record by 75 percent and establishing a record that still stands. Another outstanding career belongs to Los Angeles Laker Kareem Abdul-Jabbar. His skill, perception, and signature "skyhook" shot have earned him the award of Most Valuable Player six times, as well as *Sports Illustrated*'s Athlete of the Year for 1985.

A force to be reckoned with is the seven-foot-six Manute Bol, a former shepherd from the Sudan who plays for the Washington Bullets. The only NBA athlete ever to kill a lion with a spear, Bol heralds a new generation of professional basketball players in America recruited from foreign countries by college coaches.

The fourth of the top professional sports in the United States has roots in Canada. Hockey is a graceful interplay of agile skating with precision timing—and no qualms about rough play. The first professional competition in the National Hockey League, was in 1917; now, the league is twenty-one teams strong.

Hockey's foremost player is Wayne Gretzky of the Edmonton Oilers, a lanky skater burning up hockey records and melting the hearts of young girls across North America. Gretzky owns the records for most points in a season (212), most assists in a season (135), and most goals in a season (92). Compare these figures with Gordie Howe's twenty-six-year accumulated career records of 1,850 points, 1,049 assists, and 801 goals; check your arithmetic and believe it. To skill, strength, and speed Gretzky adds intuition, or as hockey great Phil Esposito calls it, "hockey sense," the ability to visualize where the puck will be next.

Unfortunately, hockey is a sport in which numerous heated brawls are expected, and players are penalized only slightly before they return to action. "I went to a fight," goes a famous joke, "and a hockey game broke out."

John McDonough

Scott Heiser

However, roughness and a lenient attitude toward roughness occur in other sports, too. Hard-hitting athletes win points, not to mention respect, especially in football and boxing. Green Bay Packers coach Vince Lombardi is well-known for saying, "Winning isn't everything. It's the only thing." According to writer James Michener, however, Lombardi regretted voicing this opinion, saying just before he died, "I sure as hell didn't mean for people to crush human values and morality."

Soccer is destined for growth in America, evidenced as millions of children across the country participate in youth leagues. "You've got to give these kids, seven-to-ten-year-olds, time to grow up," Don Ohlmeyer said. "The people who are watching television now, for the most part, have never played soccer. They've never seen soccer played live, and they aren't interested in soccer. It's the whole generation growing up right now that's looking at soccer as an alternative to football."

East meets west in the ongoing Celtic-Laker rivalry, left. *Did Boston Celtic Larry Bird get the ball past Los Angeles Laker Michael Cooper in this play? Professional boxers,* above, *aim for fame and fortune, but they take a pounding to achieve it.*

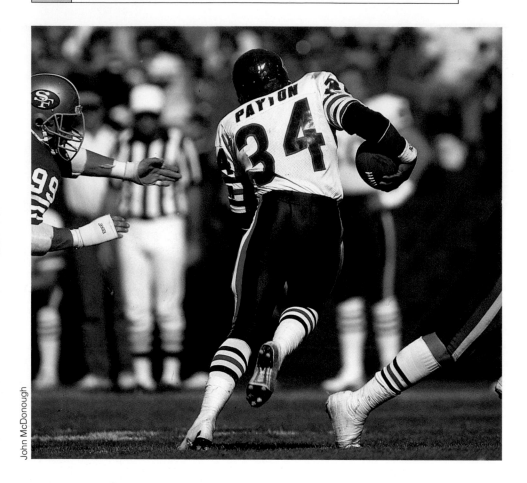

John McDonough

Walter "Sweetness" Payton, number 34 of the Chicago Bears, eludes number 99 of the San Francisco 49ers.

SALARIES

In 1984, there were twenty-two millionaires in baseball, ten millionaires in basketball, and four millionaires in football. Successful boxers are the highest-paid professional athletes, with the top prizefighters, such as "Marvelous" Marvin Hagler and Thomas "Hit Man" Hearns, making two million dollars to three million dollars and more a year. Professional hockey players make the least amount of money, "only" drawing $140,000 a year, on the average.

Baseball players rank as the second-highest-paid athletes, with some, such as Philadelphia Phillies third baseman Mike Schmidt and New York Yankee outfielder Dave Winfield, earning two million dollars a year or more. The average baseball player's salary is around $360,000. Basketball players come next in the lineup, with many earning over one million dollars a year, like the Boston Celtics' Larry Bird.

When it was created in 1982, the United States Football League raised professional football's fortune by causing a salary war with the NFL. A few USFL players earned $1.5 million a year, but NFL players are not far behind, as top athletes rake in one million dollars yearly. The average NFL salary is about two hundred thousand dollars.

Americans assume that while their heroes may be extravagant with their hard-earned money, they are honorable. Therefore, when drug use is suspected or proved, as in the well-publicized baseball cocaine trials during the summer of 1985, people lose faith in ideals. Athletes may justify drug use for relaxation, for extra energy or strength, or for thrills, but whatever the reason, drug abuse by a sports star hurts more people than just the athlete.

Baseball commissioner Peter Ueberroth is one sports official working hard to eradicate drug use. "My primary goal is to have sports figures be an example to the rest of society, because we're so visible," he said. "That means, for one thing, getting drugs out of our sports so that other parts of society can domino in that direction."

THE FUTURE

High technology has changed and sped up athletic achievements in America. Coaches use computers to work with statistics for draft selection, for probability in calling the next play, and to analyze angle, direction, force, velocity acceleration, and center of gravity for adjustment in training. Frames of film shot at a rate of ten thousand per second can be analyzed singly to pinpoint movements. Photographic equipment freezes the definitive play or time, and timing can be precise to within one one-hundreth of a second.

New equipment is introduced constantly to improve competition, from astroturf on the football field for even footing to solid (no-spoke) light bicycle wheels for less wind resistance. A microchip in the heel of some athletic footwear calibrates information while the athlete is running, and the entire shoe is later plugged into a computer for analysis.

Strong and courageous, athletes are modern American heroes who glorify the working life. Sports teach discipline, offer ideals and present entertainment, continuously astonishing and inspiring us. It's no wonder America is sports-mad.

Thousands of New York Marathon runners start the 26.2 mile journey, as seen from the top of the Verrazano-Narrows Bridge, which links Staten Island and Brooklyn.

Gayle Jann

Ranked number one and finishing first, many-times-champion Alberto Salazar sets a record at the 1982 New York Marathon.

Gayle Jann

The Randall's Island High School high jump champion shows his winning form, right.

Due in part to the attention-grabbing achievements of the American cycling team, cycling's popularity is booming across the country, below.

Gayle Jann

Steve Smith/Wheeler Pictures

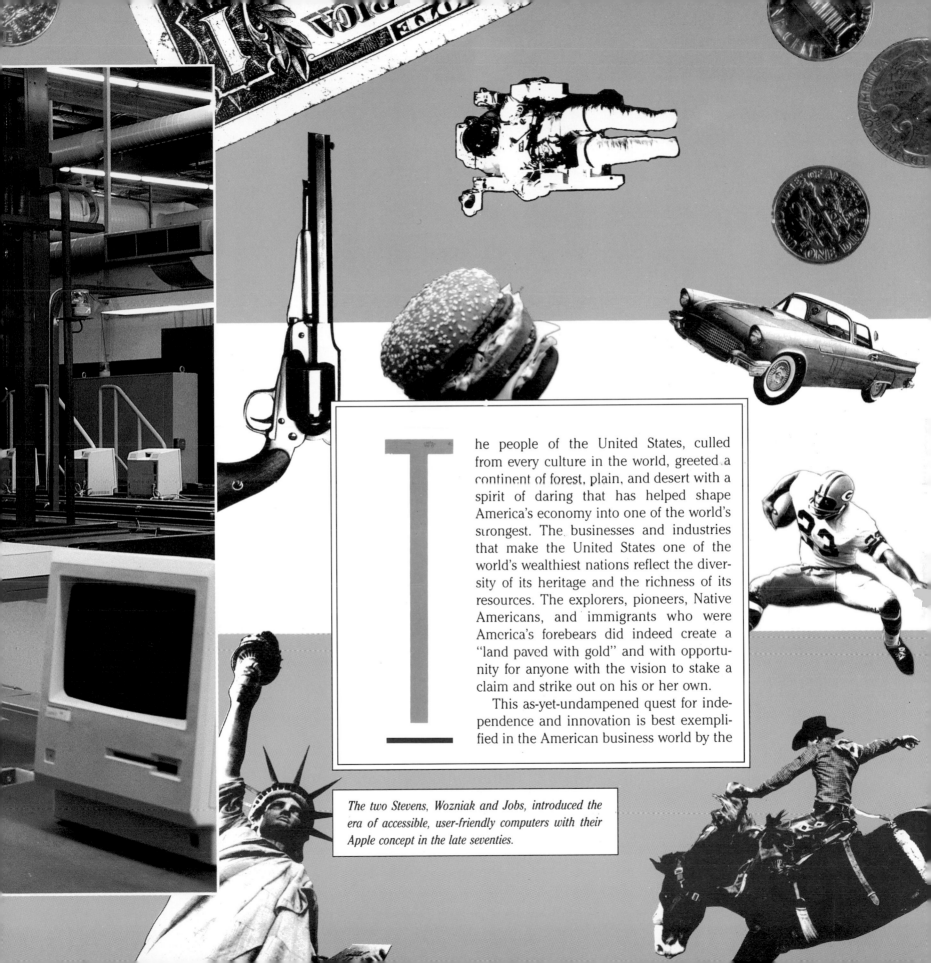

The people of the United States, culled from every culture in the world, greeted a continent of forest, plain, and desert with a spirit of daring that has helped shape America's economy into one of the world's strongest. The businesses and industries that make the United States one of the world's wealthiest nations reflect the diversity of its heritage and the richness of its resources. The explorers, pioneers, Native Americans, and immigrants who were America's forebears did indeed create a "land paved with gold" and with opportunity for anyone with the vision to stake a claim and strike out on his or her own.

This as-yet-undampened quest for independence and innovation is best exemplified in the American business world by the

The two Stevens, Wozniak and Jobs, introduced the era of accessible, user-friendly computers with their Apple concept in the late seventies.

Entrepreneurship takes many forms. This sponge shop in Key West is a prime example of making good with minimal capital, local resources, and a little bit of charm.

Sandra Dos Passos

growing number of entrepreneurs who dot the country, exploring everything from microchips in California and wood stoves in Vermont to alternative farming in Missouri. A plethora of men and women are risking financial, emotional, and physical resources when they start their own businesses in fields as varied as telecommunications, health care, bioengineering, retailing, computers and electronics, leisure and recreation, and consumer products. A new breed in American business, the entrepreneur, is striking out for economic independence in much the same way that his or her ancestors did when they came to the New World.

Though entrepreneurs are attracted to every type of business, there is no single, unequivocal description of what it takes to be an entrepreneur. By traditional standards, the definition is limited to those involved in start-up ventures and small

businesses. While many entrepreneurs get started in the world of small business, this viewpoint hardly offers a comprehensive understanding of the varied elements and motives behind entrepreneurship. Businesspeople within larger corporations, too, are taking risks and exhibiting entrepreneurial qualities as they find innovative and unconventional strategies to meet the corporations' goals.

Entrepreneurship is seen by some as the breeding ground of the New American Hero, a place where slightly superhuman individuals stretch themselves and accomplish seemingly impossible economic feats. This school of thought feels that entrepreneurs are harder-working and more community-minded than their more materially oriented colleagues. These new heros are believed to give a disproportionately large amount of time and energy to charities and worthy causes.

A less idealized view of entrepreneurship is that it's simply a small-scale version of the standard economic theory of supply and demand; if an individual applies some classic business dictums on a single, rather than corporate, level, that person is an entrepreneur. This theory proposes, for example, that anyone who hangs up a shingle and offers goods or services is engaging in entrepreneurial business. It's an inclusive definition, but hopelessly vague.

Still others believe that entrepreneurship completes the need of the "Me Generation" for self-fulfillment. This theory says that a narcissistic get-rich-quick drive fuels most entrepreneurs' desire to go solo.

Of course, none of these views is completely accurate, though there are grains of truth in each. Entrepreneurs do tend to stretch themselves more than their peers when setting and working toward a goal. And as with any business endeavor, those mavericks who are driven by the entrepreneurial dream must rely on hard economic facts that will influence their paths. The overall economic climate of the time and place, the availability of venture capital, and the ability to identify and adequately meet the needs of a market are fundamental considerations for any businessperson. Whether or not an entrepreneur is in it for the money, there's no guarantee of success. Those who do succeed, however, know that the rewards can be bountiful.

But the money and subsequent glory come at a price, sometimes a hefty one, and not everyone has what it takes to make it big—an entrepreneur must possess special qualities. As the *New York Times* has defined an entrepreneur, it "...refers not so much to the person who starts a small enterprise but to the lover of risk with the gifts to turn opportunity into success, and the businessman [or woman] who, even after amassing millions, is still driven to start another, and yet another venture." An entrepreneur, then, is someone with an insatiable need for challenge and accomplishment, someone who doesn't rest on laurels but must constantly strive for more distant horizons.

Not all entrepreneurs meet with success, however, and it must be stressed that there is no magic formula to ensure that they will. According to Peter F. Drucker, one of America's most venerated economic theorists, true entrepreneurship is a discipline, not a kiss from a Muse. Like any skill, it can be learned and mastered. Drucker's twenty-one books have been translated into twenty languages, and his status as a business guru has been unchallenged since the 1960s. It's no wonder, then, that when this sage turns his attention to entrepreneurship, people take heed.

In his book *Innovation and Entrepreneurship,* Drucker explains that innovation is the raw material of the entrepreneur, and

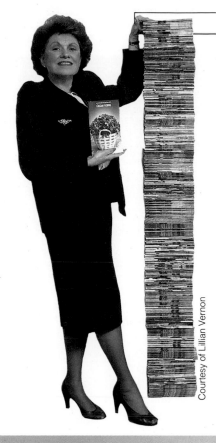

Courtesy of Lillian Vernon

"Ours Alone in All The World"—Lillian Vernon, left, *built a mail-order empire with affordable and unusual gifts and household items, often imported from around the world. Each catalogue still bears her very personal touch, one reason she's established a base of longtime, loyal customers. Bernard Goldhirsh,* below, *is the guru of current hands-on entrepreneurial trends. His Boston-based* Inc. *magazine has become required reading for business people across the country.*

Courtesy of Inc. Magazine

Bo Parker

Even within large corporations, entrepreneurship can thrive, left. Bigger, more stable companies often underwrite exploratory business ventures that can become important new areas of development. The New York Stock Exchange, below, remains the powerful financial center of the world.

Michael Melford/Wheeler Pictures

Blimps didn't have to become Goodyear's trademark—but who else do you think of when the distinctive sky boats float through the sky?

Paul B. Goode

he or she must always look for opportunities to change and institute new ideas. This can't take the form of a passive search; a true entrepreneur actively pursues possibilities for innovation.

Take, for instance, Fred Brown of Santa Barbara, California. Brown hopes his publication, *The Brown Book,* will become for used computers what *The Blue Book* is for used cars. First, however, Brown had to create a used-computer market. By starting the Microcomputer Inventory Exchange in San Francisco, Brown introduced a new idea in marketing computers. Used computers that pass through the Exchange are refurbished and sold at prices based on *The Brown Book* listings (plus a 10 percent commission).

Another creative innovator, out of Waltham, Massachusetts, is Ray Kurzweil. In June 1985, Kurzweil rolled out the world's first voice-activated typewriter. So far, the machine has a voice-recognition capacity of only one thousand words, but Kurzweil is readying a ten-thousand-word system.

Drucker also maintains that the philosophy of entrepreneurship isn't limited only to a single person or a small group of people but can involve corporations and governments as well. Much of the important risk-taking and innovation happening today, for example, is found in larger corporations, where far-thinking projects aren't mired in a swamp of financial troubles or lost in a backlog of inadequate research.

Sometimes it takes a member of a corporate community to pull the strings needed to effect change. One of America's most famous models of an industrialist-cum-entrepreneur on the cutting edge is Lee Iacocca. The son of Italian immigrants who settled in Allentown, Pennsylvania, Iacocca earned a bachelor's degree from Lehigh University and a master's from Princeton before starting work as a salesman for the Ford Motor Company. He was twenty-two.

Gourmet ice cream seems like a new trend, but it's been around for a while. Upstarts like Ben Cohen and Jerry Greenfield, however, are among the first to upset giants in the business with their distinctive flavors, top quality ingredients, and country/funky packaging.

Courtesy of Ben & Jerry's Homemade, Inc.

By the time he left in 1978, the fifty-three-year-old Iacocca was the company's president. One of his most famous contributions to Ford was the Mustang, America's first small, affordable sports car and still one of the country's most popular.

Iacocca was snapped up by Chrysler shortly after he left Ford, and supporters and detractors alike wondered why he took charge of the teetering company. Chrysler should have been equipped to cope with the troubled auto market, but when Iacocca came on board it was on the brink of financial disaster. Several factors contributed to the company's near-terminal situation: a heavy debt, outmoded production facilities, a bad subcompact recall record, and shaky overseas operations.

Behind these problems was remarkably bad management; this was the illness that Iacocca was brought in to cure. Like a ship's captain steering a cruise liner bent on an impending iceberg, Iacocca turned the company around with two particularly dramatic tactics. He approached the government with a sink-or-swim ultimatum: either Uncle Sam would give Chrysler a hefty amount of aid, or the automaker would close its doors, depriving the economy of thousands of jobs and a sizable chunk of automotive output. In a move that broke precedent and stirred national controversy—and one that saved the company—the government came through with a $1.5 billion loan guarantee. In a similarly bold step, Iacocca requested that the United States put a limit on foreign-car imports. Against all predictions, he persuaded a reluctant Congress to impose quotas. These have been credited with saving countless numbers of car-manufacturing jobs, and, almost as important, they considerably boosted the morale of the American auto industry.

While one of the country's most indus-

RCA

RCA listens to a new Master's Voice *since 1985, when General Electric bought the 80-year-old company in the biggest acquisition (outside the oil industry) in the history of business takeovers.*

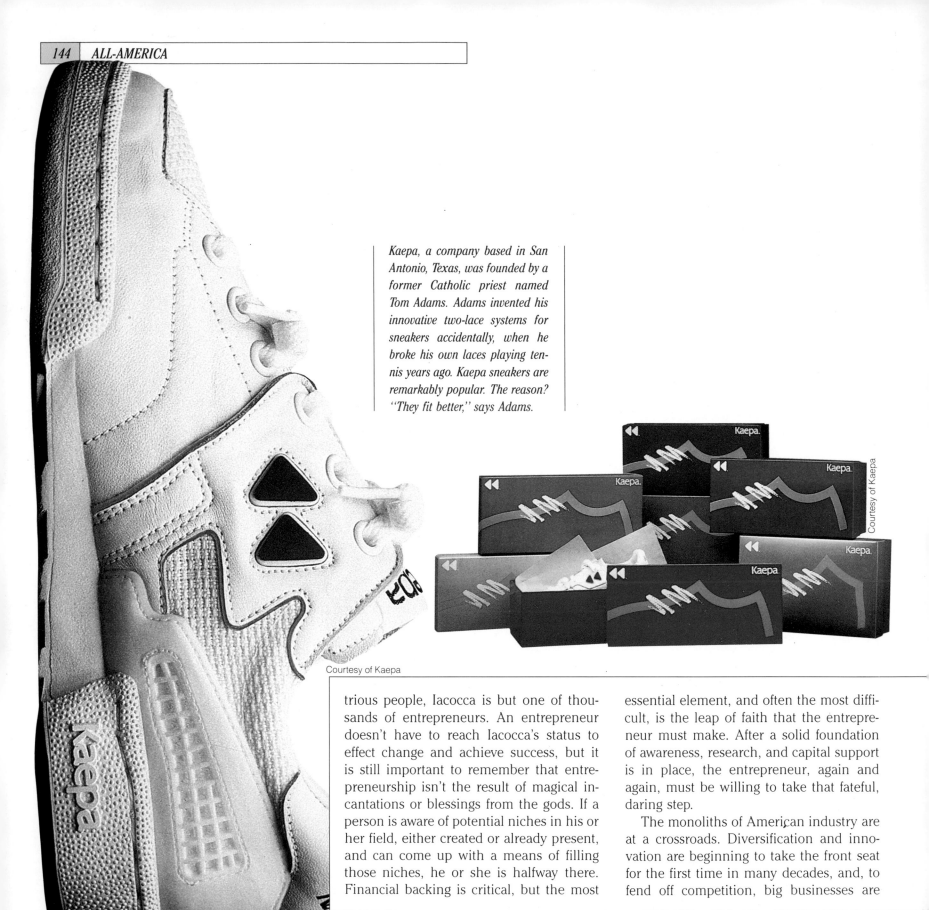

Kaepa, a company based in San Antonio, Texas, was founded by a former Catholic priest named Tom Adams. Adams invented his innovative two-lace systems for sneakers accidentally, when he broke his own laces playing tennis years ago. Kaepa sneakers are remarkably popular. The reason? "They fit better," says Adams.

Courtesy of Kaepa

Courtesy of Kaepa

trious people, Iacocca is but one of thousands of entrepreneurs. An entrepreneur doesn't have to reach Iacocca's status to effect change and achieve success, but it is still important to remember that entrepreneurship isn't the result of magical incantations or blessings from the gods. If a person is aware of potential niches in his or her field, either created or already present, and can come up with a means of filling those niches, he or she is halfway there. Financial backing is critical, but the most

essential element, and often the most difficult, is the leap of faith that the entrepreneur must make. After a solid foundation of awareness, research, and capital support is in place, the entrepreneur, again and again, must be willing to take that fateful, daring step.

The monoliths of American industry are at a crossroads. Diversification and innovation are beginning to take the front seat for the first time in many decades, and, to fend off competition, big businesses are

Two Harvard architecture students almost inadvertently started this art supply company when they bought a batch of materials wholesale and re-sold what they didn't need to their friends at a discount, left.

Southern Magazine is but the most recent and ambitious venture for publisher Alan Leveritt, a native of Little Rock, Arkansas. In 1973, he borrowed $200 in capital to start Arkansas Times magazine. Southern Magazine, dedicated to both critical reporting and quality fiction by southern writers, was successfully promoted through a direct-mail subscription campaign of 6.1 million pieces. The guaranteed initial circulation was 200,000.

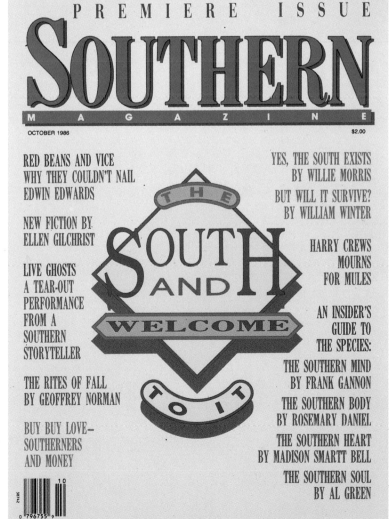

learning to incorporate not only the ideals of the entrepreneur but also the men and women themselves. New product development, distribution systems, and marketing strategies are being developed in a variety of industries. As long as the industrial and business sectors of America are willing to look beyond staid methodologies and can appreciate the promise of the entrepreneurial spirit, the country's economy will continue to show signs of growth, prosperity, and a healthy upward trend.

PERFORMING ARTS

Paula Court

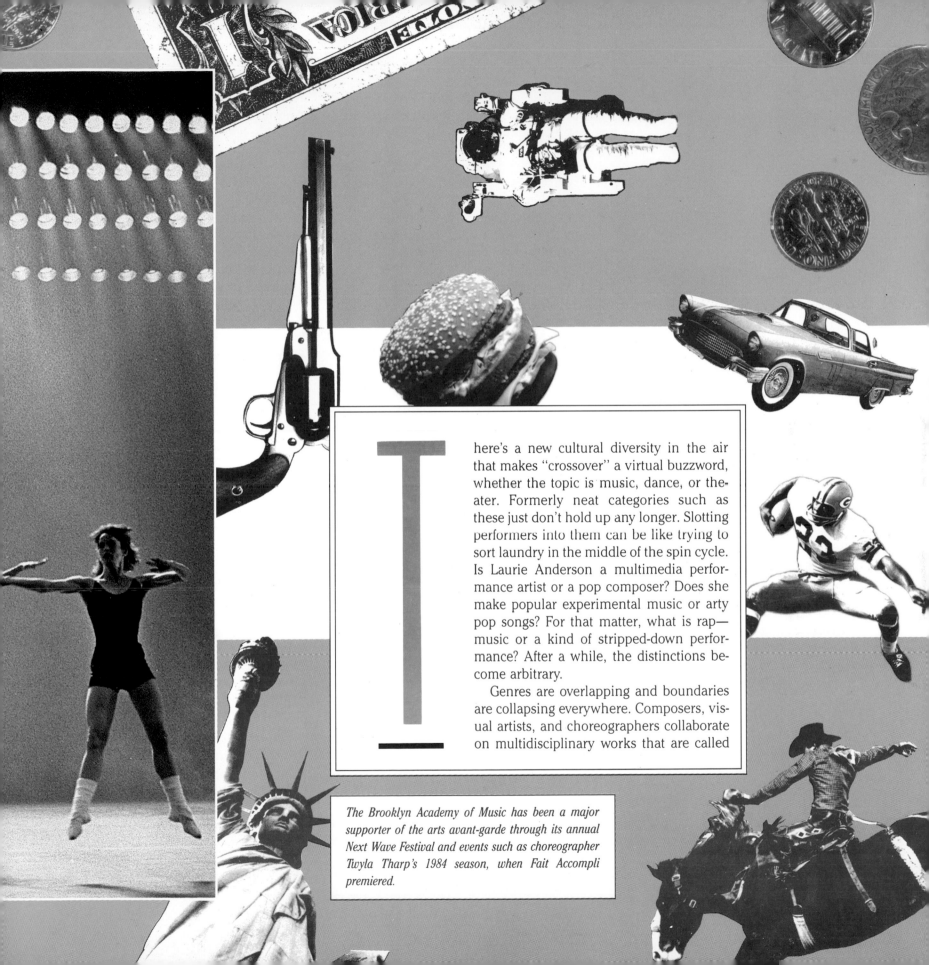

here's a new cultural diversity in the air that makes "crossover" a virtual buzzword, whether the topic is music, dance, or theater. Formerly neat categories such as these just don't hold up any longer. Slotting performers into them can be like trying to sort laundry in the middle of the spin cycle. Is Laurie Anderson a multimedia performance artist or a pop composer? Does she make popular experimental music or arty pop songs? For that matter, what is rap—music or a kind of stripped-down performance? After a while, the distinctions become arbitrary.

Genres are overlapping and boundaries are collapsing everywhere. Composers, visual artists, and choreographers collaborate on multidisciplinary works that are called

The Brooklyn Academy of Music has been a major supporter of the arts avant-garde through its annual Next Wave Festival and events such as choreographer Twyla Tharp's 1984 season, when Fait Accompli premiered.

Rap started out as a New York black street sound but the chart-topping albums of that gut-crunching rap pair, Run-DMC, pushed rap into mainstream airplay.

operas for lack of a better term. The lines between avant-garde and mainstream, high culture and pop have blurred in an unprecedented way. A generation of artists leapfrogs back and forth between what once seemed incompatible camps. For example, Sam Shepard began as an experimental playwright; now he manages to be a serious commercial playwright in addition to being a movie star.

Live performance may be just that—live—but it's also one more element in America's wider media- and technology-saturated culture. Both the media, whether TV shows or magazines, and new technology, whether Walkmans or video monitors, shape the forms live performance takes today, as well as the individual careers of performers. The movie *Koyanisquatsi* helped make the repetitive minimalism of Philip Glass's music a familiar sound with pop appeal. The crossover from live act to TV or the movies is one that guarantees many experimental or less accessible artists mainstream exposure.

Still, "the mainstream" can no longer be set up as some big, hulking monolith, just as one dominant trend or style can no longer be pinpointed. Instead, mainstream culture has become a host of competing trends, and the avant-garde just happens to be one of them. The "new" may be the vanguard of the moment, but in a media culture with a constant need for material to package and sell, anything new is just one step away from attracting pop attention. (Whoever coined the term "avant-pop" hit the mark.) All this is true, even if it does sounds a little bit cynical. Yet the crossover phenomenon is never as simple as being sucked in or selling out to the commercial culture-machine.

In this era of continual crossover, the driving, talking, rhyming beat of rap has pushed its way from black street culture into the mainstream of pop music. Rap first

came to attention along with the rest of black hip hop culture in the early 1980s. It spawned its share of white rap imitators, from Blondie, with "Rapture," to the Beastie Boys. Meanwhile, rap acts like Run-DMC and the Fat Boys have gained toeholds in the commercial music industry. If it looks as though rap has been taken over by the establishment, it keeps things in perspective to note the way rap steals in turn. Just listen to the searing heavy-metal guitars that hot whiz-kid rap producer Rick Rubin mixes behind Run-DMC's rapping. That's very definitely a part of their sound and their accessibility.

Of course, the more familiar any performance medium gets, the more popular it stands a chance of becoming. For young, second-generation rapper L.L. Cool J, the timing and the packaging are right. L.L.'s "I Can't Live Without My Radio" has broken new mainstream ground for rap. While achieving a full-scale pop crossover, L.L.'s lean, stripped-to-essentials sound also signals a new move towards minimalism, something that isn't restricted to rap. It's also in the catchy melodies and simplified instrumentals of the Talking Heads' *Little Creatures* album or even in the resurgence of solo theater performers. This isn't minimalism as Philip Glass would define it. What links these artists is a pared-down, do-it-yourself response to all the glut and garbage of a high-tech, media-filled world. Confronted with stimulation overload, they're pulling back.

Part of multimedia artist Laurie Anderson's appeal comes from her emphatically low-tech approach to the high-tech equipment she employs. Hand-drawn stick figures leap through an Anderson music video, while in her epic performance *United States I-IV,* Anderson uses her multitrack Synclavier to digitally "sample" found sounds and a harmonizer to quirkily distort her own voice. There's a folksy, alien-next-door quality to her songs, with their half-spoken lyrics, and to her be-tuxed stage presence. Her huge screen projections are reminiscent of a schoolroom demonstration. The art world accused Anderson of selling out, but she was among the first to prove that what looked like experimental performance art could be commercially successful in the pop marketplace. This edge of normalcy, and its underlying message of accessibility, no doubt helped propel Anderson to her current pop-star status and mass appeal.

Anderson has taken the next big step toward mainstream accessibility and gone to the movies with a documentary-cum-concert film, *Home of the Brave.* She's not the only art musician to turn toward Hollywood, either. David Byrne of the Talking Heads got behind the camera to direct a feature film, *True Stories.* Byrne epitomizes the new crossover chameleon, as he flips from movie director to arty pop star to composer of incidental music for avantgarde director Robert Wilson's mammoth, ongoing project, the opera *the CIVIL WarS.*

These days, the term composer is increasingly up for grabs. Joshua Fried calls himself a composer: This young artist uses tape loop techniques associated with experimental music to make spare, idiosyncratic songs with a pulsing dance beat. His spoken lyrics aren't derivative of rap but don't sound unlike it. Stephen Sondheim studied with art composer Milton Babbitt before he began writing highly successful but musically adventurous Broadway musicals such as *Sunday in the Park with George.* Bob Telson wrote disco hits and played with Latin bands before composing the acclaimed gospel-inspired score for *Gospel at Colonnus,* experimental director Lee Breuer's extraordinary reworking of Sophocle's Greek tragedy.

The insistently repetitive work of Philip Glass, as well as other so-called minimal-

Paula Court

Paula Court

Composer Philip Glass, above, who first put repetitive minimalism in the spotlight with his 1976 score for Robert Wilson's Einstein on the Beach, *has also composed music for Wilson's current epic the CIVIL WarS.*

Multimedia whiz Laurie Anderson, left, began as a visual artist and then became the first to prove that you could cross over from the performance art world of galleries and lofts to become a pop superstar.

ists like Steve Reich, represented a new kind of classical music when it came of age in the 1970s. The lusher, more romantic sounds of recent Reich and Glass works have gained even more mainstream exposure than before. Glass has also successfully breezed in the doors of pop culture, thanks in part to his score for *Koyanisquatsi*. He has embraced this pop status with an album featuring lyrics by pop artists ranging from David Byrne and Laurie Anderson to Paul Simon and folksinger Suzanne Vega, sung by the likes of Linda Rondstadt and the Roches.

Rock music also meets art music in an array of new ensembles that don't quite qualify as bands. These range from Glenn Branca's twelve-guitar ensemble, which creates resonating walls of sound, to young groups like one called Hugo Largo, two bass players and a vocalist who write weird, stripped-down, neoromantic pop

songs. New bands like this may have one foot in the folky, psychedelic 1960s, but their sound is firmly 1980s. They ride on the tails of melodic, regionally influenced bands like REM. Like L.L. Cool J, though, they're the voice of a new, tough minimalism that is a prevalent force today.

In the seventies, dance performances came as a clean, no-frills package with an emphasis on form. This new focus was evident in the pedestrian movements of postmodern choreographer Trisha Brown as well as in the pristine lines of modern dance master Merce Cunningham. Now dance is more likely to be seen as part of a multidisciplinary project, whether a large-scale collaboration or a young choreographer's own assemblage. Dance not only has gone high-tech, it has rediscovered the trappings of the theater. *Set and Reset*, a 1983 work by Trisha Brown, featured a score by Laurie Anderson, an elaborate set

and projections by artist Robert Rauschenberg, as well as an onstage videographer.

Collaborations like these have become a hallmark of the performing-arts vanguard. They also reflect the widespread interest in multidisciplinary work, which extends into mainstream theater and music videos. Often called opera, that being the most all-encompassing term available, these collaborations represent a new music theater, one that combines movement with scripted text, music, and striking visual effects. This was the case with the seminal work in this genre, *Einstein on the Beach,* first presented in 1976. Conceived by Robert Wilson, acclaimed for his stunning, avant-garde visual theater, *Einstein* also featured a score by Philip Glass and choreography by Lucinda Childs. The subsequent large-scale collaborations that *Einstein* helped spawn are notoriously hard to pull off, however. At times they look like nothing so

Perhaps the most original composer of Broadway musicals today, Stephen Sondheim also has a penchant for unusual subjects. Sunday in the Park With George draws on the life and work of French pointillist painter, George Seurat.

Martha Swope

much as arranged marriages between a set of trendy names.

Bill T. Jones and Arnie Zane, two younger choreographers who work together and have formed their own company, demonstrate the way contemporary dance has embraced theatricality with renewed vigor and with successful results. Their collaborative *Secret Pastures* included costumes by fashion designer Willi Smith and a set with a movable tent and large cutouts by pop artist Keith Haring. *Secret Pastures* also showcased Jones' and Zane's characteristically hair-raising choreography. The way the dancers hurl their bodies energetically and fearlessly through the air underscores the fact that this performance is *live*. Jones and Zane may be interested in theatricality, but not in illusion. Instead, their work highlights a riskiness and intensity that cannot be reproduced.

Risk and acrobatic athleticism: That's where what might be best called "new dance" is heading. Yet current cultural eclecticism ensures that new dance also encompasses Seattle's Mark Morris, who adapts a modern-dance vocabulary and often choreographs to classical scores to create streamlined, passionately human work.

Both Morris and the Jones/Zane duo have crossed from downtown lofts to larger mainstream audiences. Similarly, modern dance's Twyla Tharp not only choreographed the movie *Hair* and the Broadway restaging of *Singin' in the Rain*, but at the other end of the spectrum has created several works for the New York City Ballet. Jones and Zane, both of whom have been noted for and accused of having a hip, pop-oriented sensibility, have their eye on Broadway, too. Like many younger artists, neither Tharp nor Jones and Zane consider that expanding their audience makes them less serious choreographers.

Then there is classically trained Karole Armitage, who danced George Balanchine

Martha Swope

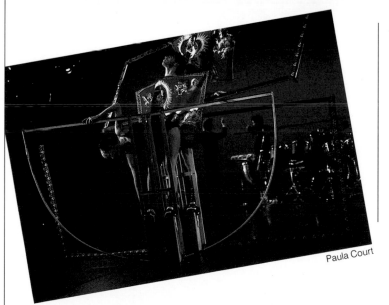

Paula Court

Twyla Tharp typifies the new kind of cultural eclecticism. She has choreographed the remake of the musical, Singin' in the Rain *for Broadway, above, as well as impassioned, athletic pieces for her own modern dance company to scores by such young contemporary composers as David Byrne, Glenn Branca, and David Van Tiegham.*

Karole Armitage's Watteau Duets *offers a radical, highly charged inversion of male/female dance pairings, performed to a throbbing live score.*

Paul B. Goode

*Under artistic director Mikhail Baryshnikov, the reper-
toire of the American Ballet Theatre ranges from
classics such as* Swan Lake *to works by Postmodern
choreographers Karole Armitage and David Gordon,
below.*

*Comedy provides a meeting
ground: Lily Tomlin may be
called a comedienne but her work
bears many similarities to that of
solo performance artists such as
Eric Bogosion.*

Martha Swope

ballets and performed with Merce Cunningham's company before breaking away
to create her own work, which is filled with
stylish but radically distorted classical
movement and often set to aggressively
loud, post-punk scores. Now, after being
discovered by Mikhail Baryshnikov, Armitage is choreographing for the American
Ballet Theatre. However, a prodigal daugh-
ter isn't simply returning to the fold; the
classical dance world has also opened its
doors to the new dance energy that is
attracting widespread attention.

The breakdown of genres to the point
where it is no longer easy to say what is
theater and what is opera, or to separate
the avant-garde from the mainstream, has
changed the face of American theater, too.
The extremely high budgets necessary to
produce the classic Broadway show have
greatly diminished the number and quality
of offerings there. The neon lights of Times
Square and the spectacle of a big production lure many to watch yet another cast of
costumes twirling, dancing, and singing.
However, the significant producers today
find the big budget format prohibitive, so
they've moved away from Broadway, and
even from New York.

It's far more representative to turn to
Peter Sellars, who used to be the head of
the American National Theatre at the Kennedy Center in Washington, D.C. Sellars,
who has directed everything from Handel
operas to Brecht to a Herbie Hancock music video, set the pace for a generation that
grew up on rock music and TV and takes
cultural diversity for granted.

This new pluralism in contemporary
theater is geographic, too. If heads don't
automatically turn to Broadway, they don't
even necessarily turn to New York. There's
a growing emphasis on regional theaters
or, if the term regional seems derogatory,
then resident theaters across the country—
from the LaJolla Playhouse in California to

Boston's American Repertory Theatre. Theaters like these not only develop new playwrights but, as important, also produce strong ensembles of actors, who may go off to Broadway or to the movies but don't abandon their theatrical origins. For them, Broadway or Hollywood no longer represent one-way tickets to the Big Time.

The Steppenwolf Theater Company of Chicago has become synonymous with the current breed of ensembles as well as the attendant emphasis on ensemble acting, rather than star turns, that this engenders. (The ensemble emphasis is evident even in the movies. Think of *The Big Chill* gang or the brat pack of *Breakfast Club* fame.) Steppenwolf didn't coalesce around a theater but around a group of scrappy actors just out of college who formed their own company, took on directing responsibilities, and staged acclaimed, gritty, forceful productions of Sam Shepard's *True West* and Lanford Wilson's *Balm in Gilead,* among other works. These plays, fitting comfortably within the hip mainstream, are the kind of tough, naturalistic, recent American dramas the company favors.

While Steppenwolf members Laurie Metcalf, Glenne Headly, and Gary Sinise have established independent acting careers, they won't quit the Steppenwolf pack. John Malkovich directed and acted in the Steppenwolf production of *True West.* The attention he attracted led to a part opposite Dustin Hoffman in Arthur Miller's *Death of a Salesman* on Broadway as well as movie roles. In spite of his expanded reputation, however, Malkovich still returns to act and direct with Steppenwolf.

Peter Sellars brought the Steppenwolf company to the Kennedy Center, but he also invited to this bastion of serious, mainstream culture a very different kind of ensemble. New York's Wooster Group falls decidedly within the arts vanguard. Yet its singular, high-tech, hyperactive produc-

tions—some generated from autobiographical material, others radical reinterpretations of texts from Flaubert to Arthur Miller—have brought the group increasing attention from the mainstream theater community. Now the group has begun to work with outside directors such as Sellars and Richard Foreman. Writer and director Foreman's own career swings back and forth between the avant-garde spectacles of his Ontological-Hysteric theater company and the commercial world.

If the Wooster Group's work is more experimental than Steppenwolf's, this didn't stop group member Spalding Gray, who pursues an independent career as a startling autobiographical monologuist, from ending up, like John Malkovich, in the movie *The Killing Fields.* Other Wooster Group members have appeared on TV's "Miami Vice" or gone the Hollywood route, too. Leaps of this kind seem to be happening all the time. From the avant-garde to prime time isn't that far at all.

Pop culture and avant-garde fragmentation combine in the work of John Jesurun. He's one of the high-caliber, enduring talents to explode out of New York's East Village club scene, an early eighties hotbed for experimental performance. Jesurun's plays have juxtaposed dialogue with lyrics from rock songs, taken the serial form of a TV series and turned it into theater, and recreated filmic devices, such as overhead shots, with economical wit on stage. A man standing against a piece of white board is to be seen as a man lying on the floor. Jesurun's scripts may push verbal dislocation to dizzying extremes as well, but they're always delivered by identifiable characters. But then, this strangely skewed dialogue is also as close to the mainstream as the hyper-realistic style of David Mamet's acclaimed Broadway production *Glengarry Glen Ross.*

Or what about the seventeen-year-old

Martha Swope

Director Mike Nichols discovered Whoopi Goldberg performing at New York's downtown Dance Theatre Workshop and brought her to Broadway. Now Goldberg pursues a career in the movies.

Paula Court

performance artist on Broadway—if you count comedienne Lily Tomlin playing a seventeen-year-old performance artist in her solo show *The Search for Signs of Intelligent Life in the Universe,* written by Jane Wagner. There's a whole genre of solo performance art that feeds off and feeds into mainstream comedy, which in any case often has a slightly subversive relationship to whatever it takes aim at. The links between the two obviously go both ways. "Where's the line between them?" Tomlin seems to be asking. She flips between characters as if pressing a TV remote-control button, zapping from one to another in midstride. This kind of fragmentation wouldn't look out of place on stage at a tiny downtown club.

Whoopi Goldberg, whose roots are in San Francisco's experimental theater community, is another new-breed crossover artist who has speedily ended up a movie star. Her *Spook Show,* a series of hilarious, wrenching portraits ranging from a junkie to a black six-year-old who wants blond hair, played smaller houses until director Mike Nichols took a chance and brought

Paula Court

Goldberg to Broadway. Mainstream acclaim led to a starring role in Steven Spielberg's movie *The Color Purple.*

Eric Bogosian still gets called a performance artist although it's his roots in the downtown New York art scene more than anything else that now separate him from Tomlin, the Hollywood and TV veteran. Bogosian's solo shows, such as *Drinking in America,* combine social satire with hilarity. Like Goldberg's characters, Bogosian's coked-out movie agents and destructive young thugs aim at pushing their characters beyond stereotypes to inspire uneasy, self-revelatory laughter.

In this high-tech age, there is an unending supply of mediated news and entertainment. A world of TVs and Walkmans has not succeeded in making live performance outmoded, however. Live energy isn't reproducible—although a concert can't replace the privacy of listening to a record at home. The new eclecticism, which values both, should act as a stimulation. And if performers can switch between "Miami Vice" and experimental theater, there's no reason why audiences can't, too.

The collaborations of choreographer Merce Cunningham and composer John Cage over the past 23 years have made them seminal figures for today's generation of artists.

SCIENCE AND INVENTION

Courtesy of NASA

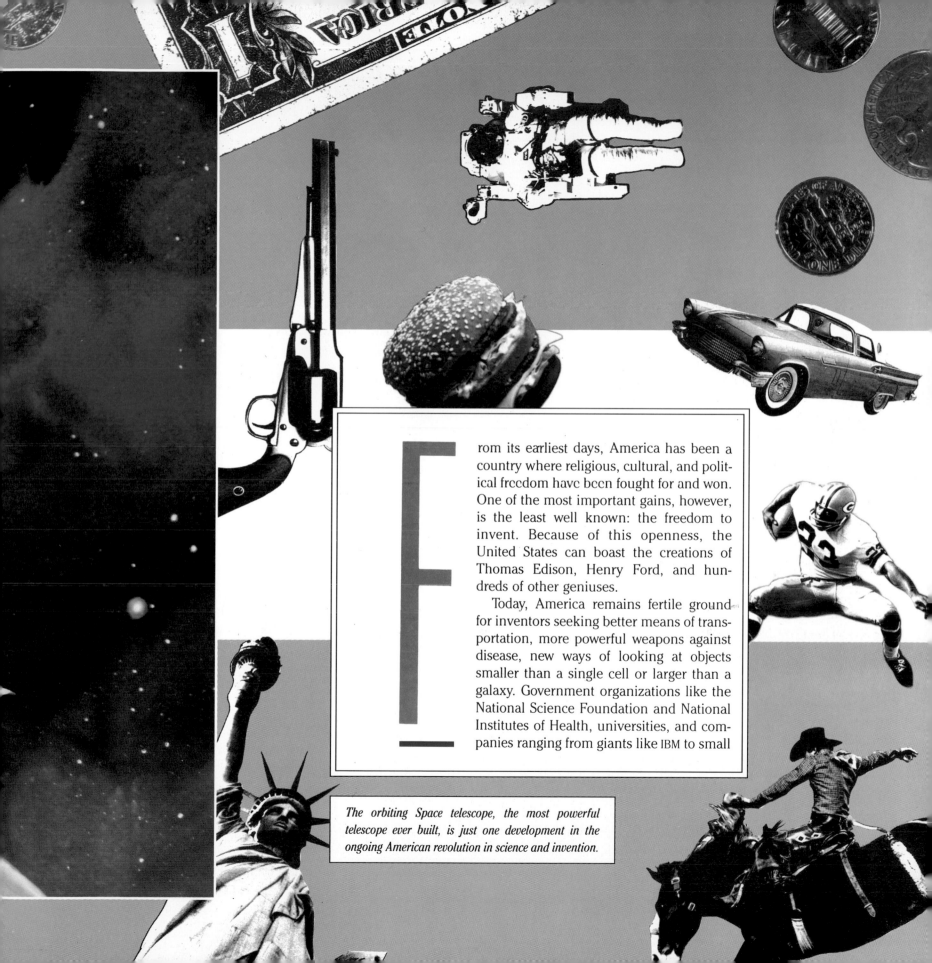

From its earliest days, America has been a country where religious, cultural, and political freedom have been fought for and won. One of the most important gains, however, is the least well known: the freedom to invent. Because of this openness, the United States can boast the creations of Thomas Edison, Henry Ford, and hundreds of other geniuses.

Today, America remains fertile ground for inventors seeking better means of transportation, more powerful weapons against disease, new ways of looking at objects smaller than a single cell or larger than a galaxy. Government organizations like the National Science Foundation and National Institutes of Health, universities, and companies ranging from giants like IBM to small

The orbiting Space telescope, the most powerful telescope ever built, is just one development in the ongoing American revolution in science and invention.

Library of Congress

Microscopes have long helped doctors discover important new weapons in the fight against cancer and other deadly diseases. The scanning electron microscope (SEM), below, *can magnify cells, viruses, and other tiny objects 50,000 times.*

International Scientific Instruments, Inc.

entrepreneurial firms are all devoting enormous energy to research and development. Their efforts are allowing us to cross frontiers that would have been unimaginable just a few years ago.

INNER AND OUTER SPACE

One such frontier is the microworld, and the vehicle that still carries researchers there is the microscope, first invented more than 400 years ago. From its primitive beginnings, it helped biologists discover the structure of living things and enabled Louis Pasteur and others to prove that illness could be caused by outside organisms. By the beginning of this century, U.S. optical companies were producing lenses that gave images of superb quality, yet the simple compound microscope remained a severely limited tool—and eventually its limits were reached.

Technology's great leap forward was the development of electron microscopes. Perfected in the 1950s in the United States and Europe, these instruments focus an intense beam of electrons on an object to produce an image of extraordinarily high resolution and unheard-of magnification. Most impressive is the scanning electron microscope (SEM), which bounces the electron beam off the surface of an object that has been coated with a metallic film. The resulting image, magnified tens of thousands of times, seems three-dimensional, tiny crystals resemble great, towering castles, while minuscule mites loom like monsters from a nightmare.

The problem with SEMs is that they can only magnify an object that's been coated with metal, a procedure that obviously doesn't allow the viewing of a living creature. With this in mind, scientists at the Massachusetts Institute of Technology came up with a technique that doesn't sacrifice the victim. The living organism is enclosed in a chamber whose walls have tiny perforations, then the electron beam is shot through the holes. The object is rotated under the beam, and the resulting image decoded by a computer and projected onto a video screen. Thus, the smallest details of cells and other living things can be viewed, seemingly in three dimensions and at magnifications exceeding fifty thousand times.

Microscopes that rely on other new techniques are also being developed, many by American-based computer companies, which use them to inspect microchips. IBM, for example, has recently designed several new instruments, including ones that use lasers and ultrasound, to produce clear, high-contrast images. And equally exciting is a new microscope that substitutes a proton beam for electrons, thus producing both an image of unparalleled clarity and precise measurements of an object's chemical composition.

But perhaps most important is the growing use of microscopes in tandem with powerful computers. This marriage of technologies, already found in hospitals and research institutions across the United States, helps doctors diagnose illness far more quickly and accurately than ever before. Louis Pasteur and other early microscope enthusiasts would surely approve.

While the SEM and other instruments are helping biologists understand the complex structures of the microworld, a slew of new telescopes is providing the same excitement for astronomers in observatories in California, Hawaii, Arizona, and other states. These complex devices are helping scientists probe nearby planets and distant galaxies—and even answer some crucial questions about the universe's creation.

Library of Congress

New telescopes use computers, not the human eye, to see X-rays, radio waves, and other parts of the previously "invisible" universe. The Space Telescope, below, can travel close to nearby planets, distant galaxies, and to the edge of the Universe itself.

Courtesy of NASA

The Voyager *spacecraft captured these glorious views of Saturn.*

Astronomers have long had the ability to build powerful light-gathering telescopes. Unfortunately, these are now considered to be of very limited use, as many celestial objects emit no visible light but rather X-rays, radio waves, and ultraviolet and infrared radiation. For, as long as we were scanning the skies through traditional telescopes, we were blind to a vast universe right before our eyes.

Astronomers have now begun to unveil instruments capable of penetrating the barriers that cloaked so much of the heavens. In 1978, the International Ultraviolet Explorer (IUE), built by the United States and several European allies, was launched into orbit; now it searches for mysterious ultraviolet rays blocked by the earth's atmosphere and relays reams of information to satellite stations scattered across the globe. Similarly, in 1983 the Infrared Astronomical Satellite (IRAS) pinpointed a "star nursery" and spotted signs that Vega, a nearby star, may support planets.

But perhaps the United States' two greatest accomplishments in astronomy are the continuing saga of the Voyager 2, a spacecraft which is taking us to the end of our solar system, and the Space Telescope, an orbiting device that allows us to see to the very edges of the universe. Both will help answer questions that have puzzled scientists for generations.

The Voyager 2 spacecraft was one of a pair launched in 1977 to visit Jupiter and Saturn and view those huge planets and their many moons. The mission was a spectacular success; the images the craft sent back are still engraved in the minds of millions of amateur astronomers. But Voyager 2 didn't stop working; using the gravity of the large planets as a slingshot, it continued its flight toward the outer reaches of our solar system. It provided the first close-up views of Uranus, discovering delicate rings and ten new moons circling that little-known world. And it travels onward to encounter Neptune—the last and most mysterious of the large planets. Nearly every bit of information it sends back is new.

The Space Telescope, designed by scientists across the country, won't jaunt across the solar system. During its orbits around earth, however, this multipurpose instrument—the most ambitious program in space-science history—gathers data that makes most all other telescopes seem like primitive toys. It is a light-gathering telescope that brings our galaxy, and the universe itself, into far sharper focus than was ever possible before.

Among the instruments the Space Telescope carries is a Faint-Object Camera, able to photograph objects twenty thousand times fainter than those visible to the naked eye; the Wide Field/Planetary Camera, which provides unparalleled views of distant planets; and a High-Speed Photometer, which makes it possible to examine puzzling light variations in stars. Most important, the telescope peers deeper into space than any previous instrument. With it, we are able to look seven times further and study a remarkable 350 times more stars than we can with other telescopes.

The farthest of these stars may provide us with answers to the question that continues to intrigue American scientists and the public alike: How was the universe created? The light we see through the Space Telescope was emitted by stars fourteen billion years ago, when scientists think the universe was newly born. No one can predict what such echoes from the unimaginable past will tell us, but one thing is sure: The Space Telescope carries astronomers and stargazers alike into regions never before explored except in the realms of science fiction.

THE DEEP FRONTIER

In the relentless drive to map the world, one area has long been neglected, even forgotten: the ocean floor, which covers more than two-thirds of the earth's surface. However, many American scientists have taken on the challenge to develop the tools to explore this unfamiliar frontier, to pry the grudging secrets from the deep sea.

The shallow areas on the ocean's edges have been comparatively well-studied, though surprising new discoveries continue to turn up. For instance, *Alvin,* a tiny

Rod Catanach, W.H.O.I.

Computer-run, remote operated vehicles (ROVs) like this one, left, *designed by California's Hydro Products, use robot hands to perform delicate tasks deep beneath the sea.*

Alvin, above, *a three-person submersible that carries scientists to uncharted areas of the deep-sea floor, discovered an unknown animal community that existed half a mile under water.*

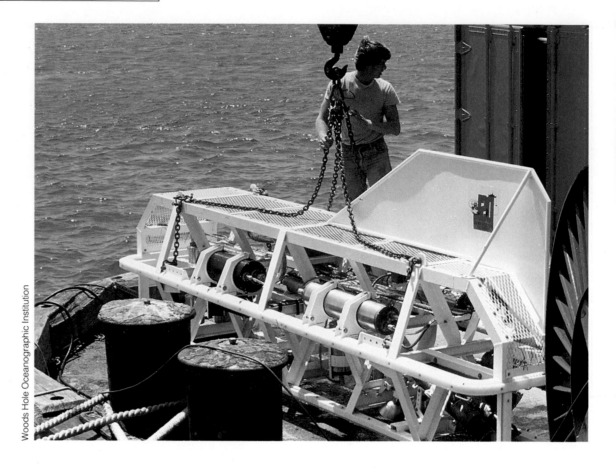

Woods Hole Oceanographic Institution

The unmanned Argo, *operated by scientists on the surface and equipped with video cameras, discovered the wreck of the* Titanic *lying more than two miles below the surface.*

three-person submersible operated by the Woods Hole Oceanographic Institution (WHOI) in Massachusetts, uncovered a community of previously unknown living creatures off the coast of California.

Yet, it is the deep-sea floor that fascinates most American oceanographers. Throughout the world's ocean lie vast expanses of unseen land averaging more than thirteen thousand feet in depth—far deeper than any manned vehicle can descend. To explore this forbidding territory, WHOI and other American oceanographic institutes have begun to design submersibles that can journey across the ocean floor alone, relaying information to scientists waiting aboard ships on the surface.

By far the most famous submersible is *Argo,* the small craft that helped discover the wreck of the *Titanic* lying more than

two miles deep. Developed by WHOI and attached by a cable to a ship on the surface, *Argo* is towed 120 feet above the seafloor and sends back detailed images along a cable with its wide-angle film and television cameras.

Argo's companion vessel (named *Jason,* of course) will come equipped with a variety of sensitive instruments, including video cameras and delicate grasping arms. *Jason,* tethered to *Argo,* will detach from the larger sub and investigate anything interesting down below, catching deep-sea creatures or analyzing the composition of the water or the seafloor itself.

Jason will be a more versatile and powerful cousin to a new breed of submersibles called remotely operated vehicles (ROVs), hundreds of which have been built for scientific research and industrial use by

Florida's Perry Offshore, California's Ametekstraza, and dozens of other U.S. companies in the last few years. Most of these computer-operated submersibles come equipped with robot arms designed to collect samples, gather lost gear, or undertake other delicate tasks at depths up to six thousand feet.

The next generation of submersibles, that will offer even greater scientific advances, is also approaching. EAVE-East, designed by scientists at the University of New Hampshire, contains five microcomputers that will enable the craft to operate without a cable to send and receive data. Its computers will allow EAVE to chart its own progress, negotiate obstacles, and gather information. If testing is successful, a new wave of independent deep-sea robots is guaranteed to follow.

LIFE WITH ROBOTS

The robot arms that many ROVs sport are just one example of America's most successful technology. For decades, robots could be found only in books and science fiction films. In the seventies, the first simple devices, designed to tighten bolts and do other repetitive jobs, began to appear in factories. However, with more than fifteen thousand industrial robots laboring in the United States alone—and others undertaking complex tasks not dreamed of a few years ago—the age of the robot has definitely arrived.

Most American industrial robots remain single-use mechanical arms that help build cars in factories. But new dexterity, sophisticated sensors, and computer-based "intelligence" enable others to assume a far more important role in manufacturing. Many can now be found in the computer and other high-tech industries, inserting complex parts into equipment, determining if a piece is broken or out of place, and calling for human help when needed.

But the true robot revolution can be seen outside of the factories. Thousands of Americans have bought home robots, those cute little humanoid machines, decked out with flashing lights, that trundle about fashionable living rooms coast to coast. These comparatively primitive devices (perhaps the best known is the Heath Company's "Hero Jr.") aren't good for much else than as conversation pieces, but they do show how familiar we've grown with robots in a short time.

Mobile robots, often equipped with hydraulic arms, scanning video cameras and public-address systems, are put to better use by many U.S. police departments. These robots carry bombs and other haz-

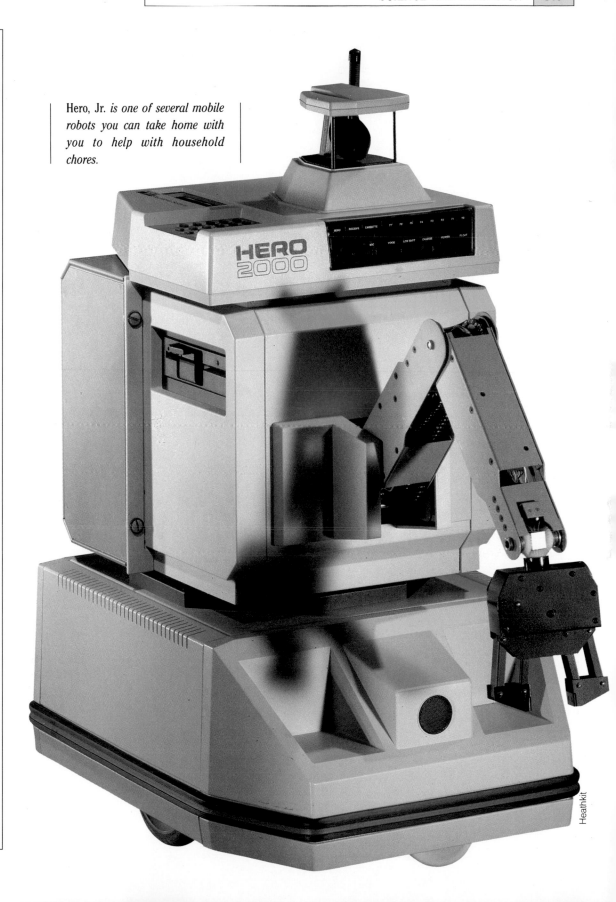

Hero, Jr. *is one of several mobile robots you can take home with you to help with household chores.*

Heathkit

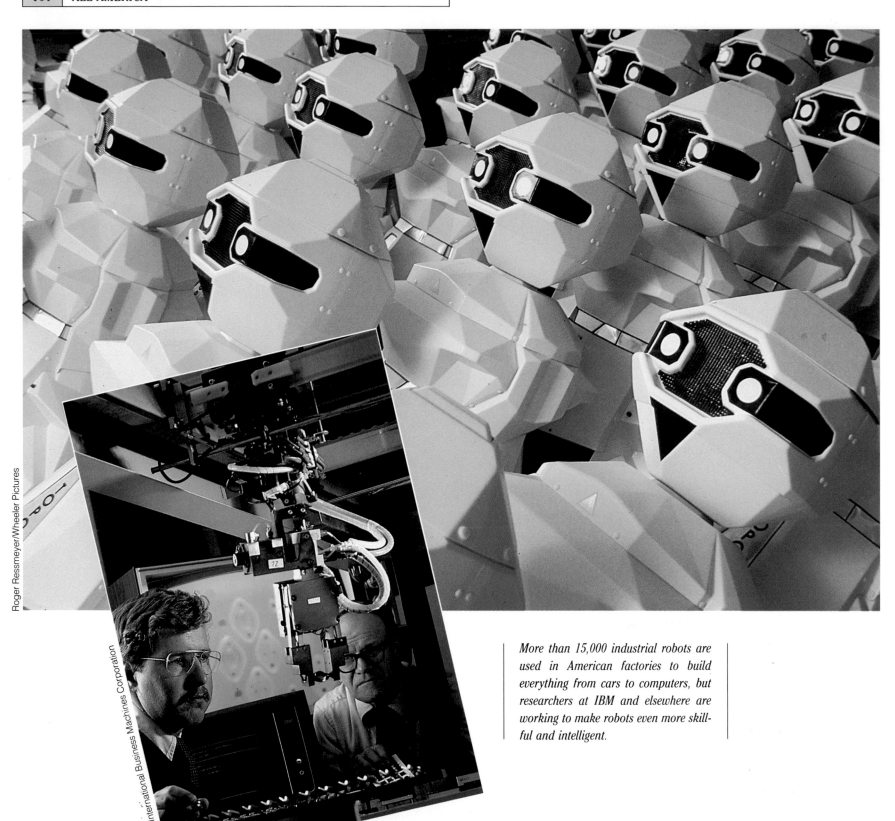

Roger Ressmeyer/Wheeler Pictures

Courtesy of International Business Machines Corporation

More than 15,000 industrial robots are used in American factories to build everything from cars to computers, but researchers at IBM and elsewhere are working to make robots even more skillful and intelligent.

ardous substances to safe locations, allow police to view crime scenes from a distance, and open communication between officials and criminals in hostage crises.

A more dramatic form of law-enforcement robot has been designed by a Massachusetts firm called Denning Mobile Robotics. Their computerized sentry can be programmed to patrol warehouses or prisons, reporting anyone trying to break in or out. A far more chilling entry on the security scene is named Prowler. Created by Robot Defense Systems in Colorado, this robot tank is designed to guard such strategically important areas as military installations; it will carry sensors enabling it to locate intruders—and machine guns and grenade launchers to effectively deal with unwelcome visitors.

On a more encouraging note, robots can be found not just building cars or protecting property, but also saving lives. At California's Memorial Medical Center of Long Beach, for example, surgeons are using a remarkably versatile computer-driven robot arm to perform biopsies on patients suffering from brain tumors. This new robot (christened Ole) comes equipped with a microcomputer to control each of its six joints, providing unmatched precision and versatility. With the help of a CT scan (an extremely detailed and accurate X-ray), the robot's computers calculate the exact location of a tumor, then order the arm to swivel into place. Surgeons can then insert a long needle through a tiny incision in the skull to reach and biopsy the tumor. The procedure, which was once frighteningly risky and often required major surgery and a long hospital stay, with robotic assistance takes only a short time, and the patient is allowed to go home the next day.

Yik San Kwoh, Ole's designer at Memorial Medical Center, believes the robot will soon be used to drain dangerous brain abcesses or even to implant radioactive material to fight inoperable cancers from within. Meanwhile, other surgical robots are also beginning to arrive. One such robot positions a patient's limb during arthroscopic surgery—on voice command from a nearby doctor.

MEDICINE

American research and development efforts have long made the United States the world's leader in medical technology. Today's medical marvels range from a diagnostic device so bulky and expensive that it can be found in only a few hospitals and clinics to a take-home pregnancy test that costs less than twenty dollars. Americans are finding that advanced medicine is making the fight to stay healthy a little easier.

The hulking diagnostic tool, catchily dubbed Magnetic Resonance Imaging (MRI), is one of the main reasons why. This machine makes X-rays and other techniques seem primitive. And it operates on principles that seem plucked straight from the world of fantasy. Scientists have long known that the nuclei of some atoms in the body exert a tiny magnetic force. MRI, by producing a magnetic field ten thousand times that of the earth's, forces these nuclei to line up in one direction (much as every compass needle in America points north). A burst of radio waves then causes the nuclei to jump out of line. When the burst stops, they resume formation—and release their own minuscule pulse of radio waves, each type of cell setting off a different signal. MRI's computers use these waves to produce an ultraprecise map of the area being scanned. This complex technique can pinpoint tiny blood clots in the brain before they develop into life-threatening strokes, locate previously invisible lesions in the spinal column, and detect the pres-

Robert Landau

Not too long ago, Americans depended on potions hawked by traveling "doctors" to treat illness. Today, new high-tech inventions are making health care far easier and more effective.

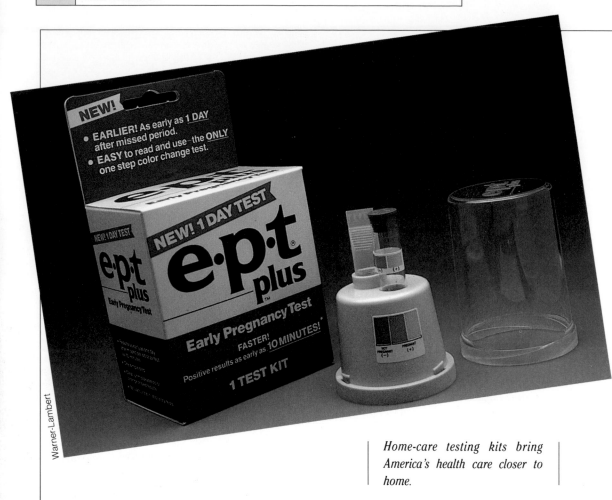

Warner-Lambert

Home-care testing kits bring America's health care closer to home.

portant American trend in medicine. Millions of people are choosing to use kits to check themselves for conditions ranging from venereal disease to pregnancy—and do-it-yourself tests have become a billion-dollar business.

Among the most widely used kits are blood-sugar monitors for diabetics. Many of these depend on sensitive strips that change color to indicate glucose levels, but others feature battery-powered meters with digital readouts and hand-held computers that diagnose the exact dose of insulin needed, taking into account contributing factors such as exercise.

Home-care test kits have also been introduced to detect possible colo-rectal cancer, breast disease, urinary-tract infections, and gonorrhea. All share one characteristic that makes them particularly attractive to users: easy-to-read results, usually consisting of a reactive strip or solution that changes color to indicate a positive test. Most are considered to be relatively accurate, although none is a substitute for a real physician if there's any doubt.

By far the most popular kits are those that tell a woman her peak period of fertility and those that inform her if she's become pregnant. Like many other tests, they depend on a fascinating new substance known as monoclonal antibodies. These are proteins, secreted by cells, that have the ability to bind to such molecules as enzymes or hormones. Although their existence has long been known, it took some time for scientists to figure out how to isolate and produce monoclonals that would bind to specific, previously targeted molecules. The home-test boom has monoclonals to thank for its success.

Among the kits that depend on this technique is Warner-Lambert's "e.p.t.-plus," a pregnancy test containing a monoclonal that binds to human chorionic gonadotropin (HGC), a hormone that women produce

ence of damaged areas in the heart and lungs. Most exciting of all, MRI may become invaluable in providing early detection of such killers as breast and lung cancer.

The MRI isn't the only futuristic device on the market. According to many physicians, laser technology is an increasingly useful method of combating a wide variety of diseases. These lasers aren't the destructive beams of intense red light so familiar to fans of James Bond and *Star Wars*. The excimer laser, for example, is the world's first cool laser, using ultraviolet light and gases to break down molecules without heat. Other lasers destroy tumors photochemically by the use of organic dyes.

Lasers are used to refasten detached retinas and relieve the symptoms of glaucoma in eye patients, remove brain and spinal-cord tumors that require painstakingly precise surgery, and destroy kidney and gallbladder stones. Experts believe that a special type of excimer laser may soon function as a virtual vacuum cleaner for clogged arteries. Using a laser attached to a catheter and fiber-optic lens, a surgeon will be able to patrol a patient's arteries, searching for fatty buildup. A quick burst from the laser will disintegrate any blockages—and a future of inexorable heart disease will have been avoided.

Far less ambitious than MRI or lasers and less expensive than a visit to many doctors, home medical tests may be the most im-

after becoming pregnant. Urine is added to a solution containing a bright red dye; if HGC is present, it will bind to the monoclonals, causing the solution to turn nearly clear. This simple test, according to its producers, is reliable more than 90 percent of the time, a far higher success rate than previously available home tests. Other pregnancy tests work similarly, as do tests to determine fertility, which use monoclonals to target human leutinizing hormone, a substance that surges a day or so before ovulation.

While monoclonal antibodies are a driving force behind the home-test boom, they are also proving helpful to doctors seeking to treat patients more effectively in the office or hospital. Products to detect the presence and location of heart disease or tumors are already under development. Next, physicians may be able to tag monoclonals with toxic substances, which will then attack the tumor cells that attracted the antibodies. This technique may some day be a potent weapon against cancer.

It is said that, a century or so ago, an eminent businessman recommended that all American patent offices be shut down indefinitely. They were no longer necessary, he explained, because everything had already been invented. Luckily, his idea wasn't adopted, and soon the automobile, electricity, and other inventions proved him to be wrong.

No one would make a similar mistake in America today. Such devices as robots that aid in surgery, telescopes that look to the edge of the universe, ships that sail the deepest sea, and countless others are a tribute both to their inventors and to America's continuing position as a leader in all branches of science and technology. That position, unchallenged almost since the country's beginnings, continues to serve both its residents and the rest of the world unquestionably well.

From the inside of a cell to the edge of a distant galaxy, America's technological innovations are leading to unimagined scientific frontiers.

Courtesy of NASA

ENTERTAINMENT AND LEISURE

Robert Landau

echnological advances throughout our country, indeed throughout our world, have affected virtually every aspect of American life. Improved transportation and communication, longer paid vacations, shorter work weeks, and labor-saving gadgets in our industries, businesses, farms, and homes have provided Americans with more of that coveted gem—spare time. Never known to sit back and snooze while a party is going on, Americans have certainly been using their extra time to the best of their entertaining abilities.

FAIRS AND FESTIVALS

Attending fairs has undoubtedly become one of America's most enjoyable pastimes. Nearly 130 million

Peals of laughter and shrieks of terror ring out from youngsters defying the laws of gravity on the latest ride at the county fair, while others are attracted to the ferris wheel—the fair's first "main attraction."

Keith Glasgow

Sandra Dos Passos

One charming little girl, above, enjoys a visit to the balloon man at the fair, while others, above right, look on as farm animals pass by. Balloons, prize livestock, and the rodeo are key ingredients of the fair. A cowboy, below, demonstrates his horsemanship and his skill with a rope before a crowd of local well-wishers.

Robert Landau

people a year attend state, regional, or country fairs—more people than attend professional football games. Beginning as cattle and sheep shows for farmers, fairs eventually grew into large-scale events (especially after the appearance of the Ferris wheel) that featured the latest inventions, carnival rides, and competitions. Although the Berkshire Agricultural Society held a food and livestock exhibition in Pittsfield, Massachusetts, in 1810, the very first state fair is generally considered to have been held in Syracuse, New York, in 1841. Michigan, running a close second, held one eight years later in 1849.

For a while, fairs attracted families and children who gathered for community, fun and relaxation before the busy harvest season. As time went on, however, the event also attracted local and national politicians, horse racing, and, along with that, gambling. This bleak period, when the fair was known more for corruption than as a forum for farmers, was short-lived, and the original intentions of the fair—attention and respect to farmers—eventually were restored.

Livestock shows, farm-machinery exhibits, contests, concerts, freak shows, delicious homemade food, and community involvement are the ingredients of a good American state fair. Communities and individuals alike begin preparations months in advance, and the fair holds a number of events that are eagerly awaited by participants and spectators. Contestants bone up on their hog calling; prize tomatoes are nurtured from the seed to the can; and cows and sheep are fed, groomed, and fussed over almost as if they were young children being readied for their first day of school—save for the fattening up.

Many fairs across the country offer other forms of entertainment. The Kansas fair, for example, features foreign-trade exhibits that display the latest products and inventions of foreign countries, invited annually by the state. The larger state fairs often have a grandstand stage with new musical acts appearing each year. Iowa's fair is certainly one of the most famous, thanks to the many versions of the popular movie *State Fair* set in Iowa. In addition to this notoriety, Iowa has one of the largest livestock shows; featuring more than seventeen thousand animals, the show needs a twenty-acre spread to display all the farm machinery. A variety of contests and games from egg rolls, footraces, bike races, and piggyback rides for children to best tomatoes, best pies, and other culinary contests for connoisseurs of home cooking make state fairs a big attraction for people of diverse ages and interests.

Festivals are another form of celebration and entertainment that often include many fair-type activities, but usually focus on, or highlight, one particular aspect of American culture and society. Whether in honor of a local community's past, like the Anchorage Alaska Fur Festival, or in tribute to an entire nation's heritage, like the 1986 Statue of Liberty Celebration, these events are testament to Americans' appetite for entertainment.

In the northeastern United States, for example, foliage festivals and tours are held to celebrate the exquisite colors of autumn. From the end of September through October, the trees, in vivid shades of gold, red, and green, beautifully change the face of the northeastern landscape, and each year millions of Americans flock to the area to witness the phenomenon. These festivals, which are held in every state in New England, are usually weeklong events that also feature art and antique shows, contests, tournaments, dances, and parades.

The coastal areas of the United States and the Gulf of Mexico are known for celebrations of their fishing and boating heritages. Since August 1947, Rockland, Maine, has held the Maine Seafood Festival, where locals lay claim to the "World's Largest Lobster Boiler." The boiler can "stomach" as much as eight hundred pounds of lobster in each of its two hatches. Every year, more than six thousand seafood dinners are served during the festival. The festival also includes a parade, coastal-oriented arts and crafts, square dancing, fireworks, and a midway. On the West Coast just north of San Francisco, in Bodega Bay, the Annual Fisherman's Festival features a colorful sea parade that follows the time-honored tradition of blessing the fishing fleet. Nearly one hundred boats decorated with balloons, streamers, and flags pass along the waterfront to be reviewed. Arts-and-crafts fairs, music and "bathtub" races—races with homemade boats made from milk cartons, spare wood, and the like—are also scheduled events.

The festival for which the South is most noted is the Pre-Lenten Carnival or Mardi Gras in New Orleans. It's one of the best examples of America's penchant for lively parties that can last for days on end. At the same time, it represents a tradition that, although it has been modified a little over the years, refuses to die. For more than a century, each year in the weeks before Lent, all-male clubs from New Orleans' oldest families have formed krewes (crews) to build floats and stage parades and balls. A new king and queen are crowned every year, and the identities of the male krewe members are hidden. After the parades, the king and queen and the rest of their court repair to very private, expensive *bal masqués*. Noted for its public spectacle and chaotic atmosphere, Mardi Gras is a time of colorful revelry, a time to whoop it up before the religious ceremonies of Lent. Traditionally, members of the krewes toss trinkets into the crowd—fake coins (called doubloons), Frisbees, and plastic beads. In addition to the parades, Mardi Gras in New

Randy O'Rourke

Keith Glasgow

Above: *At Mardi Gras in New Orleans, Louisiana, a reveler parades through the crowds dressed in typical carnival attire. The festival carries on for days at a frenzied pace, but the seeming chaos is all in good fun.* Above right: *Good rides are essential to any festive event in America, but for the more scary ones, the little girl pictured will probably have to wait until next year.*

Orleans offers the best jazz, delicious Southern cuisine, and a seemingly endless celebration that is not soon forgotten.

In the West, the cowboy and fur-trading eras are still celebrated by the Mountain Man Rendezvous or "rondys." There are at least fifty such gatherings held in eleven different states. The rondy in Jackson Hole, Wyoming is one of the best known because of its authentic flavor of the historic West. Old West Days and Mountain Man Rendezvous houses participants in twenty lodges (usually tepees and rustic lean-tos in the spirit of the Old West), and keeps festival goers entertained with a buffalo barbecue,

Indian and Western dances, and shooting events at Teton Village's Snake River Ranch. At most rondys, there's a Trader's Row where traditional items such as knives, powder horns, and hand-tanned leather clothes and bags can be purchased. Contests are informally scheduled and include 'hawk throwing, musket shooting, the telling of the tallest tale, and the viewing of the ugliest face. Don't forget your chaps when attending a rondy, because recreating the feel of the Old West is the name of the game; proper attire includes buckskins with accessories like leather pouches, powder horns, and muskets.

CULTS AND FADS

As connoisseurs of a good time, Americans have been struck by practically every mania, fad, and trend in the book. From breakdancing and Trivial Pursuit to TV subcultures and Planet Photon, we seem to be riding the crest of a new wave every other day. Nightclubs with new themes and attractions open and close virtually overnight, and, as any teenager will tell you, the music video star is one of the most transient figures in American pop culture today. Because so many things change so fast, we end up spending much of our free time either striving to be "in," "hip," and "up-to-date," or worrying that we're "out," "square," and "old hat."

This relentless fluctuation is evident in the changing tides of popular games in this country. Standard board games like Monopoly, Clue, and Password were quickly considered passé with the onslaught of video games in arcades and, later, in the home. Space Invaders, PacMan, and Galaxians, now considered video "antiques," gave way to countless other games; today, video games are produced so rapidly that shortly after they have been "born" they are rendered obsolete.

With the coming of Trivial Pursuit in our time, however, the board game has recaptured its former popularity. When the Trivial Pursuit craze first began, it was more than just a party picker-upper or something to while away the hours while it rained outside—people played the game as if they *had* to. Popular on trips, at home, at the office, and at the beach, Trivial Pursuit was everywhere. People threw Trivial Pursuit parties. In the original edition, six trivia categories asked questions in such areas as literature, history, and politics. Other editions—geared to specific age groups or interests like the Baby Boomer edition or the Silver Screen version—followed. Al-

Captain James T. Kirk, Science Officer Spock, and Dr. McCoy of the starship Enterprise *are the main reason that "Star Trek" is the most popular TV cult in the world. Fans keep the 1960s series alive in reruns and eagerly await future releases of new movies.*

though much of the initial hysteria over the game has subsided, perhaps the newest edition—Sexual Trivial Pursuit—will start a new wave of excitement.

Even the interest in video games has changed. Some video games are acted out—a "real-life" adventure. Planet Photon is one of the most popular of these games, which are usually played at converted racquetball or basketball courts or at designated areas outside. People from all age groups are now able to live out their fantasies as Luke Skywalker, Flash Gordon, or Buck Rogers. In Planet Photon, players wear helmets and battery packs and carry a kind of phaser à la "Star Trek" that shoots laser beams. The game is one of strategy, played out in semidarkness with flashing strobe lights that add a surreal, outerplanetary touch. Real-life video adventure games are popular in several parts of the country, but because of the ever-changing tides in the games market, how soon they will be replaced by the next phase in video marketing is anybody's guess.

While Americans are quick to drop one fad for another, there is also a more stable, subterranean current beneath this level of constant change—entertainment cults. Cults begin when one fan suddenly realizes that there is somebody else who shares that interest. Unlike fads, cults aren't flash-in-the-pan occurrences; they're more like long-lasting or lifetime obsessions. Determined to keep their loves alive, cult followers march in parades, write petitions, travel great distances to gather at conven-

tions, dress in cult fashion—whether it's punk, mercenary chic, or alien—and even go so far as to erect monuments in honor of cult figures. "Star Trek" followers, for example, can visit the "future birthplace" of Captain James Kirk of the starship *Enterprise* in Iowa.

The media—TV and movies in particular—have had an awesome effect on the birth and growth of cults in our society. Even if an American doesn't go to the movies, chances are he or she watches TV, owns a VCR and rents movies, or has cable TV and a movie channel. With the powerful potential of capturing imaginations, these forms of entertainment have the capability of drawing large groups of people together.

The movies *Harold and Maude*, *Rocky Horror Picture Show*, and *Rambo* all have strong cult followings. The show "Star Trek," however, has by far the largest and most vital cult in both TV and movies. Fans refused to let "Star Trek" die after the series was cancelled in the late 1960s. Created by the talented, indeed, visionary mind of Gene Roddenberry, the show was a visual *tour de force* that emphasized universal human values and represented concerns and attitudes of the times. But it is because of the cult followers, or Trekkers, that the deep and diverse world of "Star Trek" lives on. Regularly scheduled conventions, collectibles ranging from authentic phasors to Klingon paraphernalia, and fanzines with new stories and adventures all combine to make "Star Trek" a living classic and an inspiring way of life for many Americans.

AMUSEMENT PARKS

The face of amusement parks has changed dramatically since the advent of TV and other advances in America's technological environment. General amusement parks, with their assortment of rides and arcades, have had trouble keeping their heads above water and have lost their audiences to at-home entertainment. After many parks went bankrupt or simply disappeared, and after TV and technological change became a part of our daily routine, the amusement park reemerged, but this time with a new angle. Theme parks—like water parks, where there are strictly water rides and activities, or wild animal parks, like Busch Gardens, where one goes specifically for a safari-type adventure—have been far more successful than traditional parks since the 1960s. Instead of taking people for rides, theme parks claim to offer a true-to-life experience—whether it's the surf or the jungle—and tend to market the experience as an educational and fun one.

Brooklyn's Coney Island, however, is one of the few lingering exceptions to the theme park trend in amusement today. Known as "The World's Greatest Playground," it is the oldest amusement park and is also the most legendary. It has become run-down over the years but major renovation plans are under way. The park features one of the oldest and most thrilling roller coasters in the nation—the Cyclone. Legend has it that some people have been

Disneyland is one of America's favorite amusement parks. Filled with mini theme parks and thrilling rides, and shrouded in fantasy, the park's allure continues to attract millions of Americans every year.

Heinz Steenmans/Wheeler Pictures

Robert Landau

While fairs often include carnival rides as part of their overall programs, the amusement park is almost entirely made up of them. The rides get bigger and better each year and this one, right, *is guaranteed to knock your socks off, take your breath away, and make you wish you'd never left home.*

married on this famous roller coaster. Built in 1927, today the Cyclone is being restored and will move both forward and backward. As part of Coney Island's revitalization, a new baseball stadium (bringing baseball back to Brooklyn) is also being considered. The pending renovations notwithstanding, the park is still open and, in addition to its rides and arcades, visitors can stroll its famous boardwalk for beer and clams.

In keeping with the spirit of Coney Island, Six Flags Over Georgia is a giant amusement park spread out over 331 acres just outside Atlanta, Georgia. The park is divided into six sections, each one representing the six different flags that have flown over Georgia: French, Spanish, English, Confederate, American, and Georgian. Featuring more than one hundred attractions, rides, and live performances, the park has only one admission price for

everything. Popular rides include the Great Gasp, in which participants experience a forty-foot free-fall parachute drop that ends with a controlled, perfect landing; the Triple Loop Mind-Bender; the Dahlonga Runaway Mine Train; the Jean Ribaut Riverboat Adventure; and the Thunder River White Water Raft Trip.

If Coney Island is the epitome of the traditional amusement park, then Disney World/Epcot Center in Florida is the best representative of the theme park. Called a "permanent World's Fair" experience when it opened in 1982, the Epcot Center is more like several theme parks in one. Future World explores the latest technology and inventions in computers, energy, and agriculture; Spaceship Earth takes you on a journey through forty thousand years of the history of the earth; and World Showcase looks at life in different countries like Canada, France, Morocco, and China.

With over twenty-two million visitors a year, this giant park is undoubtedly the biggest tourist attraction in the world. Combining learning with adventure and family entertainment, Disney offers an unprecedented amount of fun things to do. You can meet the cast of Disney characters, Mickey and Minnie Mouse, Goofy, Pluto, and others; dine on a riverboat; journey into outer space; and enjoy haunted mansions, a tropical rain forest, theme-park rides, and penny arcades.

Disney World's ability to keep on topping itself is the main reason for the park's ongoing success. One of the grandest developments at the Epcot Center is the creation of the world's largest aquarium. Six million gallons of manufactured sea water, four thousand fish—including sharks, barracuda, and dolphin—coral reefs, and divers all make up what Disney calls The Living Seas. Now visitors can travel to the bottom of the sea for a spectacular look at life under water—and they even can dine in an underwater restaurant.

Unlike the diverse world of Disney, most theme parks offer only one theme. Water parks, for example, have cropped up in both ocean-deprived areas of the United States and in places located just ten minutes from the beach. Fans of the increasingly popular parks point out that there are no sharks, no jellyfish, and no seaweed to battle. Best of all, though the surf and rapids are artificial, they can be just as wild and thundering. Six Flags Atlantis in Hollywood, Florida, boasts sixty-five acres of water rides and a 650-foot water chute. Water enthusiasts and daredevils will enjoy the Surf Hill Ride at Vernon Valley Action Park in Vernon, New Jersey, and The Screamer at Raging Waters in San Dimas, California. Other popular water parks include Water World in Denver, Colorado, and White Water Amusement Park in Oklahoma City, Oklahoma.

Paul Morin/Photo Trends

Up Up and Away! Hot-air balloons dot the open skies with their majesty and their beauty. Balloon ascensions, both local and international attractions, are popular in the Mid-West because of the frequent clement weather and the wide open spaces. Balloonists prepare for takeoff at one ascension, above.

Sky Sports

Americans are taking to the sky more and more in their leisure time. America is a nation of sports enthusiasts in general, but sky sports in particular have become increasingly popular as technology makes them a safe, comfortable, and viable means of sporting entertainment. Hang gliding, ballooning, para-sailing, and, yes, even kite flying (the oldest form of sky sport) are modes of entertainment that embody the ideals of freedom and adventure, ideals that are appealing and akin to the American spirit.

With his kitelike sketches, Leonardo da Vinci explored the possibilities for flight as early as the Renaissance. But kite flying itself has been around for about three thousand years. Kites have been used in science, in the military, and in art. In India, kites are used for dueling in a sport called kite fighting, which is also sometimes practiced in the United States. The kite strings are coated with powdered glass, and during the duel each kite tries to cut the string of the other; the string that snaps first loses.

But, what most kite flying boils down to is simple fun. There's something about seeing a kite bob, dart, and soar in the sky above a white sand beach or a park meadow that takes one back to a simpler time. There's nothing sophisticated or snooty about kites—not even in a kite's design. Although the styles range from the basic light weight two-stick kite with paper to kites made of ripstop polyester and weighing more than one thousand pounds, no kite can be made obsolete. The experience, the frustration, and, then, the exhilarating feeling of success one has at making a kite fly is pure, unadulterated fun.

Kite flying was the inspiration for hang gliding, which was originally known as kite riding. When the hang gliding craze began, it had a reputation for being risky, a sport exclusively for daredevils. People broke arms and legs and were sometimes killed before technology stepped in to make hang gliding safer. The materials used to make the kites have improved, and hang glider pilots themselves have learned more and have refined the art and sport of flying.

Hang gliding has evolved from an experimental and adventurous activity to a sophisticated and demanding sport. The early ten-second rides have become unlimited soars over mountain tops and oceans. A sport that is also beautiful to watch, hang gliding is a triumph of spirit and mind that defies understanding of the limitations for human flight. Now there are flying sites all over the country, and, in many states, hang gliding instruction is offered for beginners.

Like hang gliding, ballooning is another sport that has had to wait for technology to catch up with it. Ballooning, also called aerostation, has been around for centuries, but in the eighties it has been made safe, cheap, and accessible.

The hot-air balloon, unlike the more dangerous kind using gas, is the ticket to the skies these days, and it seems everyone is buying one—since 1980, the number of registered balloons has more than doubled. The sport is one of the oldest forms of

The daring and thrill of adventure are undeniable aspects of any sky sport enthusiast. This hang glider, below, *is nearing the end of his journey through the skies as he approaches his landing on the dunes.*

Manuel Dos Passos

flight, and, because it is the least regulated aviation sport, it is probably the last haven for experiencing the skies in peace. Already there are several ballooning events, and the number of festivals increases every year. At festivals, balloons compete in "hare and hound" races and in precision altitude-keeping.

In the family of sky sports, para-sailing is ballooning's second cousin. The latest variation on the sky sport theme, it is popular on the beaches of vacation spots like southern Florida and along the California coast. Gliding high and free through the air in a parachute, the para-sailer is pulled along by a boat in the water. Para-sailing owes at least part of its heritage to Leonardo, who designed the first parachute.

Sky sport enthusiasts are increasing in numbers and are a special breed. Sky sports represent a unique combination of aesthetics and physical and intellectual skill. Even kite flying, which many regard as child's play, can be a challenge—a kite that only gets up to a thirty- to forty-degree point in the sky is considered a failure. Other aspects also set sky sports apart. It's one of the few fast-growing sports in America where profits are not a primary motivation. More important to sky sport participants are flying better, building better kites, balloons, or chutes, and avoiding government regulations—the name of the game is enjoying the open sky and doing your own thing.

Manuel Dos Passos

Para-sailers, left, *are becoming common fixtures at many festivals and resort areas as well as along many seashores. Whether you're para-sailing behind a boat or a skimobile, as pictured, you're in for a fun-filled ride. The colorful beauty of ballooning is apparent,* below, *as balloonists compete neck-and-neck in a race for the finish.*

Paul Morin/Photo Trends

GAMBLING

Right: *And they're off! A day at the races provides immeasurable excitement for all, whether you're there to bet on a horse or you just want to enjoy the race. If your luck runs out at the track, however, you can always try the bright lights of the gambling casinos,* below.

Michael Melford/Wheeler Pictures

Gambling has rarely been viewed objectively. The American public for the most part chooses sides morally and emotionally. For some, it is known as a vice, a corruption, and even a "plaything" of the devil. For many others, it is considered a passion, a sport and a science. The bottom line, however, is that gambling, for good or evil, is big business. More important, it is a thrill, and the likelihood that the gambling trend will lessen in the years to come is virtually nonexistent—or in gambling lingo, the odds of something like that occuring are at least a trillion to one.

There are several reasons why gambling is so hot in America. Basically, Americans love money. Or, perhaps gambling satisfies some kind of primitive need within people to feel in control of their lives, if only for a few moments—a feeling of power in a powerless world. The potential for a big win is too great for many Americans to pass up. But speculations aside, whether they are holding onto a handful of chips, clutching a lottery ticket, or reading a racing form, Americans find that trying to master that age-old element of chance is a good time.

More than other pastimes, gambling meets the pleasure quotas of millions of Americans, given the many forms of gambling available. In fact, avoiding the temptation is nearly impossible. Almost every state in the nation has a lottery of some sort. Betting pools based on America's other passion—sports—are popular at work, in schools, and at home.

Casino gambling, however, usually grabs the spotlight from other forms of gambling with its sparkle and celebrity style. Gambling at the casino hotels of Atlantic City and Las Vegas, two of America's most famous gaming spas, is always a grand affair. Although the casino hotels, like the MGM Grand, the Sands, or the

Keith Glasgow

Claridge, are known for catering to the serious high rollers, they also indulge many Americans who simply like to gamble in their free time. Money—not connections, prestige, or sharp clothes—seems to be the only prerequisite.

Sports betting, which is not as exclusive as casino gambling, is probably just as popular in America as sports—people are just a little quieter about it. With the advent of the personal computer, which collects and scans voluminous records and data, sports betting is being pursued with even more zeal. Of course, in addition to knowing how to use a computer, it also helps to have insight into the particular sport, a feel for developing trends, and a lot of extra free time to work on handicapping skills. Regardless of the odds, millions bet anyway. From football, hockey, and basketball to baseball and boxing, the betting opportunities are endless.

Betting at the races is similar to betting on sports and is another popular way Americans spend money. Thoroughbreds, harness racing, and even dog racing are bet on with pleasure. Thoroughbred racing is probably the most noted, however, because of the Triple Crown event—the Kentucky Derby, the Preakness, and the Belmont Stakes—which receives the most media attention. OTB, or Off-Track Betting, is a common marquee in most cities and has made betting on the races more accessible.

There are no guarantees in gambling, which is, of course, part of its appeal. It is considered by many to be a creative pursuit where opposite logic is sometimes valid. The challenge to beat the system will never die. In gambling, there's never a single, clear answer—until the end, perhaps, when the results are posted.

Americans pride themselves on knowing how to have a good time. Their reputation as rebels and risk-takers seems to hold true even in the arena of spare time. But

Atlantic City, above, *is the classic East Coast gambling center. In addition to the casinos, a gambling vacation often includes relaxing leisurely activities by the shore.*

Keith Glasgow

while they have proven themselves perfect targets for more adventuresome activities like hang gliding, gambling, or TV cults, they continue to embrace events that are steeped in tradition. Festivals have flourished, attendance at state, county, and regional fairs has increased, and amusement parks have regained their popularity. In their spare time, Americans find themselves challenging both the odds and the elements. They also have time to dress up like Klingons if they want to or time to

memorize every answer to every question in every edition of Trivial Pursuit. When the fair's in town, they manage to venture over to sample the unrivaled homemade goodies, and—just for the fun of it—some of them decide to get married on the Cyclone at Coney Island. Americans simply have an innate desire to pursue happiness, and do so by keeping themselves and the people around them entertained. The enjoyment of leisure time throughout the nation is a top priority.

SOURCES

ARCHITECTURE AND INTERIOR DESIGN

ARCHITECTS AND DESIGNERS

Antine/Polo, Ltd.
276 Lydecker Street
Englewood, NJ 07631
201–568–4862
212–690–0094

Eric Bernard Designs
177 East 94th Street
New York, NY 10128
212–876–9495

Bray-Schaible Design Inc.
80 West 40th Street
New York, NY 10018
212–354–7525

Nicholas A. Calder Interiors
348 East 58th Street
New York, NY 10022
212–308–6670

Dexter Design, Inc.
Interior Design
133 East 58th Street
New York, NY 10022
212–752–2426

Falkener-Stuetley Interiors, Ltd.
50 Pierrepont Street
Brooklyn, NY 11201
718–624–4718

Gensler & Associates
823 United Nations Plaza
Suite 500
New York, NY 10017
212–286–0212

Carolyn Guttilla/Plaza One
8 Birch Hill Road
Locust Valley, NY 11560
516–671–9280

Gwathmey Siegel & Associates
475 10th Avenue
New York, NY 10018
212–947–1240

Intradesign, Inc.
717 La Cienega Boulevard
Los Angeles, CA 90069
213–652–6114

Noel Jeffrey, Inc.
Interior Design
22 East 65th Street
New York, NY 10021
212–535–0300

Francisco Kripacz
125 North Robertson Boulevard
Los Angeles, CA 90048
213–278–1915

Richard Lawrence Associates
25 Sutton Place North
New York, NY 10022
212–752–2930

Stephen Mallory Associates, Inc.
170 East 61st Street
New York, NY 10021
212–826–6350

Robert Metzger Interiors
210 East 58th Street
New York, NY 10022
212–371–9800

Juan Montoya Design Corp.
80 Eighth Avenue
New York, NY 10011
212–242–3622

Katherine Stephens Associates, Inc.
Six Dianas Circle
Roslyn Estates, NY 11576
516–621–1460
212–764–1711

Michael Taylor Interior Design
Nine 25th Avenue North
San Francisco, CA 94121
415–668–7668

Adam D. Tihany International, Ltd.
57 East 11th Street
New York, NY 10003
212–505–2360

Calvin Tsao & Zack McKown
146 Central Park West
New York, NY 10023
212–496–0320

Rauch, Venturi & Scott Brown
40 Hudson Street
New York, NY 10014
212–608–0610

FASHION

Antique Boutique
712–714 Broadway
New York, NY 10003
212–460–8830

Barney's
Seventh Avenue & 17th Street
New York, NY 10011
212–929–9000

Henri Bendel
10 West 57th Street
New York, NY 10019
212–247–1100

Bergdorf Goodman
754 Fifth Avenue
New York, NY 10019
212–753–7300

Bloomingdale's
1000 Third Avenue
New York, NY 10022
212–355–5900

Brooks' Brothers
346 Madison Avenue
New York, NY 10017
212–682–8800

Liz Claiborne, Inc.
1441 Broadway
New York, NY 10018
212–354–4900
  accessories:
  200 Madison Avenue
  New York, NY 10016
  212–696–2500

Perry Ellis Sportswear, Inc.
575 Seventh Avenue
New York, NY 10036
212–921–8500
or
1457 Broadway
New York, NY 10036
212–921–8696

outerwear:
230 West 38th Street
New York, NY 10018
212–730–0143

Genny U.S.A. Inc.
650 Fifth Avenue
New York, NY 10019
212–245–4860

I. Magnin
830 North Michigan Avenue
Chicago, IL 60611
312–751–0500

Izod Lacoste (men's and women's)
11 Penn Plaza
New York, NY 10119
212–502–3000

Betsey Johnson
1441 Broadway
New York, NY 10018
212–921–0510

Norma Kamali
1411 Broadway
New York, NY 10018
212–944–9710

Calvin Klein, Ltd.
205 West 39th Street
New York, NY 10018
212–719–2600
  menswear
  1211 Avenue of the Americas
  New York, NY 10036
  212–730–1880

Michael Kors, Inc.
148 West 28th Street
New York, NY
212–620–4677

Ralph Lauren
33 West 55th Street
New York, NY 10019
212–977–8130

Levi Strauss & Co.
1411 Broadway
New York, NY 10018
212–704–3200

The Magnin Company
323 North Rodeo Drive
Beverly Hills, CA 90210
213–273–5910

Neiman Marcus
Main & Evoy
Dallas, TX 75202
214–741–6911

Saks Fifth Avenue
611 Fifth Avenue
New York, NY 10022
212–753–4000

The Twenty-Four Collection
2399 Northeast Second Avenue
Miami, FL 33137
305–576–6424

Keni Valenti
170 Avenue B
New York, NY 10001
212–420–8260

Wrangler (men's)
350 Fifth Avenue
New York, NY 10118
212–868–5303
  women's
  1411 Broadway
  New York, NY 10018
  212–868–5321

CONTEMPORARY CRAFTS

CRAFT GALLERIES

Adventures in Crafts Studio
51 East 93rd Street
New York, NY 10128
212–410–9373

Alaska Shop of NY, Inc.
31 East 74th Street
New York, NY 10021
212–879–1782

Ceramic Supply
10 Dell Glen
Lodi, NJ 07644
201–340–3005

Convergence Gallery
484 Broome Street
New York, NY 10013
212–226–0028

Crafts Americana
814 Lexington Avenue
New York, NY 10021
212–421–6253

Departure Gallery Ltd.
1310 Madison Avenue
New York, NY 10128
212–860–0748

Dolfinger's Inc.
325 West Walnut
Louisville, KY 40202
502–893–3634

Empire State Crafts Alliance, Inc.
Nine Vassar Street
Poughkeepsie, NY 12601
914–471–8188

Karlton Weavers
168 Fifth Avenue
New York, NY 10010
212–255–9530

M. Das Company
The Gift Center
888 Brannan Street
Suite 332
San Francisco, CA 94103
415–626–6166

Oneida Silversmiths
41 Madison Avenue
New York, NY 10010
212–684–6860

Riedel Crystal of America
24 Aero Road
Bohemia, NY 11716
516–567–7575

Rising Pottery
141 Larchmont Avenue
Larchmont, NY 10538
914–834–8827

Rope Gallery
215 Thompson Street
New York, NY 10012
212–254–7315

Signed Pieces
150 Second Avenue
New York, NY 10003
212–254–6310

Snyderman Gallery
317 South Street
Philadelphia, PA 19147
215–238–9576

Joe A. Turner
8600 Burton Way
Los Angeles, CA 90048
213–274–3020

The Works Gallery
319 South Street
Philadelphia, PA 19147
215–922–7775

FOOD AND DRINK

BREWERIES

Anheuser-Busch Inc.
One Busch Place
St. Louis, MO 63118
314-577-3314

Adolph Coors Co.
1221 Ford Street
Golden, CO 80401
303–279–6565

Miller Brewing Co.
3939 Highland Boulevard
Milwaukee, WI 53208
414–931–2000

Gennessee Brewing Co.
445 St. Paul Street
Box 762
Rochester, NY 14603
716-546-1030

Rainier Brewing Co.
3100 Airport Way South
Seattle, WA 98134
206–622–2600

F & M Schaeffer Brewing Co.
Box 2568
Allentown, PA 18001
215–395–6811

West End Brewing Co.
811 Edwards Street
Utica, NY 13502
315–732–3181

Dixie Brewing Co.
2537 Tulane Avenue
New Orleans, LA 70119
504–821–3511

GOURMET FOODS

Amana Meat Shop and Smokehouse
One Smokehouse Lane
Amana, IA 52203
319–622–3113

Balducci's
424 Avenue of the Americas
New York, NY 10011
800–228–2028, ext. 72
212–673–2600

Baldwin Hill Bakery
Baldwin Hill Road
Phillipston, MA 01331
617–249–4691

Bon Vivant
36425 Churchill Drive
Solon, OH 44139
216–248–3911

The Chocolate Catalogue
Karl Bissinger French Confections
3983 Gratiot Street
St. Louis, MO 63110
800–325–8881

Cryer Creek Kitchens
Box 1029
Corsicana, TX 75110
800–468–0088

D'Artagnan, Inc.
399 St. Paul Avenue
Jersey City, NJ 07306
201–792–0748

Dean & De Luca
121 Prince Street
New York, NY 10012
212-431-1691
  mail order:
  110 Greene Street
  Suite 304
  New York, NY 10012

Fabrique Delices
41 South Railroad Avenue
San Mateo, CA 94401
415-344-5769

Goodies from Goodman
12102 Inwood Road
Dallas, TX 75234
214-387-4804

Grandma Morgan's Gourmet Kitchen
P.O. Box 972
Lake Oswego, OR 97034
503-761-4303

Harrington's
170B-5 Main Street
Richmond, VT 05477
802-434-4444

Harry and David
Bear Creek Orchards
Medford, OR 97501
503-776-2400

Hawaiian Plantations
1311 Kalakaua Avenue
Honolulu, HI 96826
800-367-2177
808-955-8888

Manganaro Foods
488 Ninth Avenue
New York, NY 10018
212-563-5331

Oakwood Game Farm
Box 274
Princeton, MN 55371
800-328-6647
612-389-2077

Pasta Productions
12358 SW 117 Court
Miami, FL 33186
305-233-3377

Proper Puddings
912 President Street
Brooklyn, NY 11215
718-783-2486

Wisconsin Fishing Company
P. O. Box 965
Green Bay, WI 54305
414-437-3582

Zabar's
2245 Broadway
New York, NY 10024
800-221-3347
212-787-2000

RESTAURANTS

Abbott's Lobster in the Rough
117 Pearl Street
Noank, CT 06850
203-536-7719

Beal's Lobster Pier
Clark's Point Road
Southwest Harbor, ME 04679
207-244-3202

Bob Sykes Bar-B-Que
1724 Ninth Avenue
Rte. 11
Bessemer, AL 35023
205-426-1400

Bookbinders
215 South 15th Street
Philadelphia, PA 19102
215-545-1137

Cassell's Patio Hamburgers
3300 West Sixth Street
Los Angeles, CA 90020
213-480-8668

Catfish 'N'
Dardanelle Dam Road
Dardanelle, AR 72834
501-229-3321

Chez Hélène
1540 North Robertson Street
New Orleans, LA 70116
504-947-9155

The Chili Bowl
220 Fredericksburg Road
San Antonio, TX 78201
512-732-0406

El Cacique
125 Duvall Street
Key West, FL 33040
305-294-4000

The Four Seasons
99 East 52nd Street
New York, NY 10022
212-754-9494

Galatoire's
209 Bourbon Street
New Orleans, LA 70130
504-525-2021

Grand Central Oyster Bar
42nd Street & Vanderbilt Avenue
New York, NY 10017
212-490-6650

Junior's
386 Flatbush Avenue
Brooklyn, NY 11238
718-852-5257

Katz's
205 East Houston Street at Ludlow
New York, NY 10002
212-254-2246

Mammy's Kitchen
Highway 17 South
Savannah, GA 31408
712-945-6007

The Orange Inn
7400 East Coast Highway
Rte. 101
Corona del Mar, CA 91720
714-644-5411

Original Joe's
301 South First Street
San Jose, CA 95113
408-292-7030

Tad's Chicken 'N' Dumplings
Rte. 30
Troutdale, OR 97060
503-666-5337

Union Oyster House
41 Union Street
Boston, MA 02108
617-227-2750

Vermont Sugar House
Jcts. of Rtes. 14 & 107
Royalton, VT 05068
302-763-8809

WINES AND LIQUORS

Almaden Vineyards
1530 Blossom Hill Road
San Jose, CA 95118
408-269-1312

Bacardi Corp.
Box 3549
San Juan, PR 00936-6207
809-795-1560

James B. Beam Distilling Co.
500 North Michigan Avenue
Chicago, IL 60611
312-527-9500

Black Prince Distillery
691 Clifton Avenue
Clifton, NJ 07011
201-365-2050

Brookside Vineyard Co.
2801 Guasti Road
Guasti, CA 91743
714-983-2787

California Growers Wineries
2238 41st Avenue
San Francisco, CA 94116
415-398-1111

Jack Daniel Distillery
Box 199
Lynchburg, TN 37352
615-759-4221

Delicato Vineyards
12001 South Highway 99
Manteca, CA 95336
209-289-1215

E & J Gallo Winery
600 Yosemite Boulevard
Modesto, CA 93354
209-526-3111

Guild Wineries & Distilleries
500 Sansome Street
Box 27846
Concord, CA 94527
415-798-7722

Royal Crown Co., Inc.
Drawer K
Miami Beach, FL 33141
404-394-6120

Joseph E. Seagram & Sons, Inc.
375 Park Avenue
New York, NY 10152-0001
212-572-7000

D.G. Yuengling & Sons Inc.
Fifth & Mahantongs Street
Pottsville, PA 17901
717-622-4141

FILM, TELEVISION, AND RADIO

AUDIO AND VIDEO EQUIPMENT

Acoustat Corporation
3101 SW First Terrace
Fort Lauderdale, FL 33315

Acoustical Physics Labs
151 Sixth Street, NW
Atlanta, GA 30313

Acoustic Design Group
P. O. Box G3
Aspen, CO 81612

ADC, Audio Dynamics Corp.
Division BSR, USA, Ltd.
Pickett District Road
New Milford, CT 06776

Advent Division International,
  Jensen Inc., and Esmark Co.
4136 North United Parkway
Schiller Park, IL 60176

B & W Loudspeakers, Ltd.
Anglo-American Audio
286 Brentwood Drive
Hudson, OH 44236

BASF Systems, BASF Wyandotte Corp.
10 Crosby Drive
Bedford, MA 01730

Cerwin-Vega, Inc.
12250 Montague Street
Arieta, CA 91331

CM Labs
8000 Madison Pike
Madison, AL 35758

DBX Inc.
Rte. 303
Blauvelt, NY 10913

Electrocompaniet
P. O. Box 173
Holis, ME 04042

General Electric Corp.
(For product information, call
1–800–626–2000)

Gott Labs
424 Clay Pitts Road
East Northport, NY 11731

GTE, Sylvania, Inc.
1000 Huyler Street
Teterboro, NJ 07608

Hammond Industries
8000 Madison Pike
Madison, AL 35758

Infinity Systems, Inc.
7930 Deering Avenue
Canoga Park, CA 91304

Lancer Electronics
18350B Ward Street
Fountain Valley, CA 92708

Microfidelity
14 Van Zant Street
Norwalk, CT 06855

Panasonic
One Panasonic Way
Secaucus, NJ 07094

Pioneer Systems, Inc.
230 Fifth Avenue
New York, NY 10001

RCA Consumer Electronics
600 North Sherman Drive
Indianapolis, IN 46201

Zenith Radio Corp.
1000 Milwaukee Avenue
Glenview, IL 60025

FINE ARTS

ART MUSEUMS AND GALLERIES

Art Institute of Chicago
Michigan Avenue at Adams Street
Chicago, IL 60603
312–443–3600

Mary Boone Gallery
417 West Broadway
New York, NY 10013
212–431–1818

Brooklyn Museum
Eastern Parkway
Brooklyn, NY 11238
718–638–5000

Leo Castelli Gallery
420 West Broadway
New York, NY 10012
212–431–5160

Dallas Museum of Fine Arts
1717 North Harwood Street
Dallas, TX 75226
214–421–4188

Gracie Mansion Gallery
167 Avenue A
New York, NY 10009
212–477–7331

Kennedy Galleries, Inc.
40 West 57th Street
New York, NY 10019
212–541–9600

Knoedler Contemporary Art
19 East 70th Street
New York, NY 10021
212–794–0550

Metro Pictures
150 Greene Street
New York, NY 10012
212–925–8335

The Metropolitan Museum of Art
Fifth Avenue at 82nd Street
New York, NY 10028
212–535–7710

Museum of Modern Art
18 West 54th Street
New York, NY 10019
212–708–9400

National Gallery of Art
Fourth Street & Constitution
Avenue, NW
Washington, D.C. 20565
202–737–4215

National Museum of American Art
Smithsonian Institute
Eighth & Sixth Streets, NW
Washington, D.C. 20560
202–357–2108

Peabody Museum
Harvard University
11 Divinity Avenue
Cambridge, MA 02138
617–495–2248

Walker Art Center
Vineland Place
Minneapolis, MN 55403
612–375–7600

THE PRINTED WORD

NEWSPAPERS AND PERIODICALS

The Boston Globe
135 Morrissey Boulevard
Box 2337
Boston, MA 02107
617–929–2000

Chicago Sun-Times
401 North Wabash Avenue
Chicago, IL 60611
312–321–3000

The Daily News
220 East 42nd Street
New York, NY 10017
212–949–1234

Kiplinger Washington Letter
1729 H Street, NW
Washington, D.C. 20006
202–298–6400

Minneapolis Star & Tribune
425 Portland Avenue
Minneapolis, MN 55415
612–372–4141

The New York Times
229 West 43rd Street
New York, NY 10036–3913
212–556–1234

Newsweek
444 Madison Avenue
New York, NY 10022
212-350-2000

People
1271 Avenue of the Americas
New York, NY 10020
212–586–1212

The Saturday Evening Post
1100 Waterway Boulevard
Indianapolis, IN 46202
317–634–1100

Time, Inc.
1271 Avenue of the Americas
New York, NY 10020
212–586–1212

US
215 Lexington Avenue
New York, NY 10016
212–340–7500

USA Today
1860 Broadway
New York, NY 10023
212–265–6680

The Wall Street Journal
22 Cortlandt Street
New York, NY 10007–3107
212–285–5000

The Washington Post
1150 15th Street, NW
Washington, D.C. 20005
202–334–6000

SPORTS

Amateur Softball Association
   of America
2801 NE 50th Street
Oklahoma City, OK 73111
405–424–5266

American Bowling Congress
5301 South 76th Street
Greendale, WI 53129
414–421–6400

American Hanggliding Association
P. O. Box 66306
Los Angeles, CA 90066
213–390–3065

American Kitefliers Association
Macleans, VA 22101
703–821–3228

American Hockey League
218 Memorial Avenue
Box 100
West Springfield, MA 01090
413–781–2030

Babe Ruth Baseball
1770 Brunswick Avenue
Trenton, NJ 08648
609–695–l434

Balloon Federation of America
2516 Hiawatha Drive, NE
Albuquerque, NM 87112

Golden Gloves Association of America
1316 East 22nd Street
Des Moines, IA 503l7
515–262–3345

Int'l Pro Rodeo Association
Box 615
Palus Valley, OK 73075
405–238–6488

National Basketball Association
645 Fifth Avenue
New York, NY 10022
212–826–7000

National Football League
410 Park Avenue
New York, NY 10022
212–758–1500

People-to-People Sports Committee
98 Cutter Mill Road
Great Neck, NY 11021
516–482–5158

American League of Professional
   Baseball
350 Park Avenue
New York, NY 10022
212–371–7600

Jockey Club
380 Madison Avenue
New York, NY 10017
212–599–1919

U.S. Golf Association
Golf House
Far Hills, NJ 07931
201–234–2300

PERFORMING ARTS

THEATERS

American Ballet Theatre
890 Broadway
New York, NY 10003
212–477–3030

American National Theatre & Academy
246 West 44th Street
New York, NY 10036
212–921–2990

American Theatre of Actors
314 West 54th Street
New York, NY 10019
212–581–3044

Brooklyn Academy of Music
30 Lafayette Avenue
Brooklyn, NY 11217
718–636–4100

Carnegie Hall
881 Seventh Avenue
New York, NY 10019
212–903–9700

The Kennedy Center for the
   Performing Arts
Alliance for Arts Education
Washington, DC 20566

La Jolla Theatre
904 Silverado Street
La Jolla, CA 92037

Lincoln Center for the Performing Arts
140 West 65th Street
New York, NY 10023
212–877–1800

   Alice Tully Hall
   194l Broadway
   212–362–1900

   Avery Fisher Hall
   Broadway at 65th Street
   212–580–8700

The Julliard School
144 West 66th Street
212–799–5000

The Metropolitan Opera House
Lincoln Center Plaza
212–799–3100

New York City Ballet
Lincoln Center Plaza
New York, NY 10023
212–370–5677

SCIENCE AND INVENTION

SCIENCE MUSEUMS

Neil Armstrong Air & Space Museum
Interstate Highway 75
Wapakoneta, OH 45895
419–738–8811

California Academy of Sciences
Golden Gate Park
San Francisco, CA 94118
415–221–5100

Carnegie Museum of Natural History
Carnegie Institute
4400 Forbes Avenue
Pittsburgh, PA 15213
412–622–3314

Capitol Children's Museum
300 Third Street, NE
Washington, D.C. 20002
202–543–8600

The Computer Museum
One Iron Way
Marlboro, MA 01752
617-467-4036

Museum of Science
Science Park
McGrath & O'Brien Hwys.
Boston, MA 02114
617-523-3500

American Museum of Natural History
Central Park West at 81st Street
New York, NY 10024
212-973-1300, ext. 511

National Air & Space Museum
Independence Avenue between Fourth
   & Seventh Streets, SW
Washington, D.C. 20560
202-357-1300

National Geographic Society
Explorers Hall
17th and M Streets, NW
Washington, D.C. 20036
202-857-7588

Kennedy Space Center
Visitors Center, TWA-810
Kennedy Space Center, FL 32899
305-867-1566

ENTERTAINMENT AND LEISURE

AMUSEMENT PARKS AND RECREATION

Belle Isle Aquarium
Detroit Zoological Park
P.O. Box 39
Royal Oak, MI 48068
313-398-0900

Busch Gardens—The Dark Continent
3000 Busch Boulevard
Tampa, FL 33601
813-971-8282

Carowinds Theme Park
I-77
Charlotte, NC 28202
704-588-2600

Disneyland
1313 Harbor Boulevard
Anaheim, CA 92802
818-999-5465

Knotts Berry Farm
8039 Beach Boulevard
Buena Park, CA 90620
714-827-1776

Mardi Gras
Tourist & Convention Commission
334 Royal Street
New Orleans, LA 70130
504-566-5011

Oceans of Fun
I-435, Exit 54
Kansas City, MO 64106
314-454-4444

Ringling Bros.-Barnum & Bailey Circus
3201 New Mexico Avenue, NW
Washington, D.C. 20006
202-364-5000

Six Flags Over Georgia
7561 Six Flags Boulevard at I-20
Atlanta, GA 30303
404-948-9290

Statue of Liberty Foundation
17 Battery Place
New York, NY 10004
212-422-0496
   26 Broadway
   New York, NY 10004
   212-363-3024

Statue of Liberty Gallery
525 Hudson Street
New York, NY 10014
212-929-4180

Gift Center
440 Lafayette Street
New York, NY 10007
212-477-5289

Vernon Valley Recreation
Rte. 94
Vernon, NJ 07462
201-827-2000

CASINOS AND GAMBLING

Atlantic City Raceway
Black Horse Pike
Box 1139
Atlantic City, NJ 08404
609-646-2317

Bally's Park Place Casino Hotel
Park Place at Boardwalk
Atlantic City, NJ 08401
609-340-2000

Brandywine Raceway
Box 7009
Wilmington, DE 19803
302-478-1220

California Hotel & Casino
12 Ogden Avenue
Las Vegas, NV 89101
702-385-1222

Caesar's New Jersey, Inc.
Boardwalk Regency Hotel/Casino
Atlantic City, NJ 08401
609-340-5300

Churchill Downs
700 Central Avenue
Louisville, KY 40208
504-636-3541

Claridge Hotel & Hi-Ho Casino
Indian Avenue at Boardwalk
Atlantic City, NJ 08401
609-340-3400

Fortuna Corp.
Box One
Sunland Park, NM 88063
505-589-1131

Golden Nugget
129 Fremont Street
Las Vegas, NV 89101
702-385-7111

Los Alamitos Race Course
4961 Katella Avenue
Los Alamitos, CA 90720
213-431-1361

MGM Grand Hotels, Inc.
3645 Las Vegas Boulevard
Las Vegas, NV 89109
702-739-4111

New York City Off Track Betting (OTB)
1501 Broadway
New York, NY 10036
212-221-5461

New York Racing Association
Aqueduct Race Track
Jamaica, NY 11417
718-641-4700

Playboy Hotel & Casino
2500 Boardwalk
Atlantic City, NJ 08401
609-344-4000

Boardwalk Regency
2100 Pacific Avenue
Atlantic City, NJ 08401
609-344-1520

Riverboat Casino
3473 Las Vegas Boulevard
Las Vegas, NV 89109
702-369-5000